HEALING ANXIETY

*Change Your Thoughts,
Change Your Life*

JEREMY WALKER

First published by Jeremy Walker 2025
Copyright © Jeremy Walker
Edited by Shahana Dukhi

All rights reserved. No part of this book may be used or reproduced by any means, graphic, electronic, or mechanical, including photocopying, recording, taping or by any information storage retrieval system without the written permission of the copyright owner except in the case of brief quotations embodied in critical articles and reviews.

Because of the dynamic nature of the Internet, any web addresses or links contained in this book may have changed since publication and may no longer be valid. The views expressed in this work are solely those of the author and do not necessarily reflect the views of the publisher and the publisher hereby disclaims any responsibility for them.

National Library of Australia
Cataloguing-in-Publication data:
Healing Anxiety/ Jeremy Walker

ISBN: (sc) 978-0-6484671-2-0
ISBN: (e) 978-0-6484671-3-7

general – nonfiction

CONTENTS

Forward 1
What is Anxiety? 3
High Alert 13
Stress and Anxiety 22
Self-esteem 32
People Pleasing and Boundaries 42
Obsessive Compulsive Disorders 50
Healing Your Anxiety 63
Mindfulness 75
The Power of Intention 93
Destress Options 103
Interviews, Groups and Social Confidence 118
Healing Food Anxiety 141
Sleeping Well 155
Time, Money and Energy 165
Balanced Lifestyle 181
Balanced Emotions 201
Conclusion 218

FORWARD

Anxiety is a paradox. It is a mechanism for protection, yet it often traps us, keeping us in a perpetual state of high alert. What starts as a survival instinct spirals into a misuse of imagination, creating fears of outcomes that rarely come to pass.

For those with chronic anxiety every waking moment can be a potential trigger for panic and nervous system overwhelm. The symptoms of anxiety are often mistaken for a heart attack, such is the severity. It can be very frightening.

It doesn't have to be this way.

Jeremy has been assisting people with mental health challenges for nearly two decades. In *Healing Anxiety*, he teaches through practical insights and success stories of those who are now free from anxiety's grasp. The result is a clear mind, able to reframe our thoughts rather than be overwhelmed by them.

Healing anxiety does not spontaneously happen. There are steps needed in order to achieve mindset mastery. I believe Jeremy has made a great contribution with this book. Jeremy's skill is in helping you find the underlying beliefs and fears that are causing anxiety. He will help you reframe your thoughts and direct you to more empowered thinking.

For those wanting to avoid drugs and use natural healing

solutions, this is your recovery bible. This book includes mindfulness tools and delves deep into the topics of reality, delusion, subconscious beliefs, self-esteem, OCD, confidence and healing. It's like getting 50 therapy sessions in one power-packed book.

Through storytelling, Jeremy highlights the transformative power of challenging anxious beliefs, embracing vulnerability, and discovering a middle path—one grounded in truth and balance. This is not a call for relentless positivity or denial of challenges, but an invitation to cultivate realistic, empowering thoughts that align with the reality of who we are.

At its core, this book is a guide to self-appreciation. It challenges the myths we've built about ourselves and illuminates the freedom that comes with being authentic. The reflections and practices shared here will resonate with anyone seeking to quiet the loud, intrusive thoughts of anxiety and replace them with stillness, truth, and self-mastery.

This book is a blueprint for embracing your authentic self in a world that often asks you to be anything but. It is a reminder that authenticity is not only liberating—it is healing. Through the lessons shared here, may you find the courage to step out of your illusions and into the peaceful power of your true self.

Dr John Demartini
International bestselling author of *The Values Factor*.

WHAT IS ANXIETY?

The purpose of this book is to lower your anxiety. That's the goal. Reduce how often anxiety occurs and enable you to recover quickly when it does. We will discuss the challenges that hinder recovery and the mindset that leads to freedom.

This book is open to all types of people, genders, designations, personal lifestyles, identities, nationalities, philosophies and religions. If you have anxiety, it doesn't matter what background you come from. You can change your thoughts and change your life.

Don't let anyone tell you what is right for you, including me. I will present a myriad of options that you can choose or not choose. The content described is to provide awareness of what triggers anxiety and new strategies to enhance empowered thinking.

This book assumes that you don't want to experience debilitating anxiety one day longer. This content is not about societal norms or right and wrong. My interests are in healing, truth and improving quality of life. Please receive the messages herein with this intention.

The stories might provide a flash of awareness or an idea. Please feel free to write these down. From a practical standpoint taking notes helps us remember more than reading alone. One of the great joys in my life has been discovering hidden knowledge that helps myself and others. I hope you enjoy this too.

Stories about myself and clients are factual, allowing that small details change with memory. The integrity of the case studies is intact. Names have been changed to ensure privacy and some details were condensed for the purpose of being brief.

My intention is that this book is highly useful and relevant for you. I have balanced being thorough, with making this content practical. There are anxiety reduction tools you can use immediately and refer back to when needed. Anxiety is complex, so we are going to break it down into smaller components like thoughts, beliefs and nervous system interaction.

Throughout we will discuss safety, confidence, healthy self-esteem, truth and balance which are at the centre of psychological freedom. Some insights will be mind-expanding, allowing you to see the bigger picture. Other ideas will provide deeper understanding of your subconscious mind, leading to self-acceptance and self-control. All are important while you craft a mindset that does not resist, nor fear anxiety but is capable of progressing beyond it.

Progress will come by choosing healing instead of fear. Recovery from anxiety needs to be the most important thing in our life, more than the million things we feel we have to do, or be. It needs to be the number one priority. We don't have to tolerate things detrimental for our wellness, including our own thoughts.

What if I get afraid of healing? Important question. We don't fear healing, we fear trying to get better and failing. Anxiety is the trickster that creates doubt. The focus is still on the negative. Acknowledge that healing is a wonderful opportunity for you. Admit that you really do want to heal and are tired of doubt and self-judgement.

At any time our thoughts are either helpful or harmful, true or untrue. Be conscious of which is present and choose healing thoughts going forward. Thought patterns that increases safety, make you present, bring self-acceptance and boost confidence can be treasured. Every though counts.

In truth, healing is a way of being, not a single event of change. I suggest, thinking and acting in ways that promote wellness and make sense for your life goals. Whilst mindfulness strategies can be useful for everyone, consider your personal circumstances.

This book is for individuals, couples and families wanting to free themselves from anxiety. Safety is the number one factor at all times. Reach out to your medical, legal, therapeutic and accounting professional for guidance when considering a life change. The suggestions are not a replacement for professional advice that takes into account your unique situation and circumstances.

DRUGS NOTE

This book will not recommend drugs, alcohol and medication to control anxiety, because of the side-effect risk. My position is to offer tools for self-regulation and deal with the fears behind anxiety. All suggestions herein are for well-being of the body and empowerment for the mind.

Others may agree or disagree. My life work so far is to trust the body and mind to heal itself. There may be no need to submit to side-effect risk in order to heal. Careful consideration should be given to your chosen healing path. Before trying medication, it's worth reflecting on these questions:

- Is there a clear stress at work or at home that needs addressing?
- Have mindfulness processes (rhythmic breathing and healing self-talk) been given a chance to work?
- Have healing methods such as correcting self-talk and therapy been given a chance to work?
- Does the habit of worrying need to be addressed?
- Is there a toxic environment or person to seek distance from?
- Has healing work been undertaken to build healthy self-esteem?

If considering medication, it's worth asking your doctor these questions:

- Why is this medication being prescribed?
- What are the effects and side-effects of this drug?
- How long before the medication starts to be effective?
- What are the risks and withdrawal symptoms when I stop taking it? How long will that last?
- Are there effects on sleep, appetite, mood, nausea, dizziness, ability to work, clarity of mind, weight gain/loss?
- Can you recommend a Hypnotherapist, Psychologist, Demartini Method or CBT practitioner?
- What other options are available?

Be aware of the benefits and limitations of treatment options. A reliance on medication to do all the healing work is unrealistic.

Some of my clients consider taking medication and nicotine patches while quitting smoking with hypnotherapy. I mention that, "It is not my place to prescribe specific medication advice, just that it will be difficult to know what worked if you do several treatments at once. I would rather the healing credit goes to the power of your own mind."

There is trust in your subconscious mind once you learn to self-regulate.

Be in charge of your mental health. If your health professional doesn't consider safe treatment for your anxiety disorder, then seek out one who does. If they are not current on treatment options, get another opinion. You deserve help from someone who has your holistic well-being in mind.

I wouldn't wish for anyone to risk the delicate balance of chemicals in their brain to a random medication. Is your Doctor confident the drug will create healing? Can they confirm it is safer and more effective than Hypnotherapy, Demartini Method, Psychology, Naturopathy, Acupuncture and Tai Chi?

WHAT IS ANXIETY?

Anxiety is felt throughout the body, including the chest, stomach, throat and jaw. It can be accompanied with symptoms such as: nervousness, shortness of breath, tightness, headaches, panic, tingling, numbness and sweating. Butterflies in the stomach, teeth grinding, nail biting and undereating or overeating are common when anxious.

Anxiety can have several components. Social anxiety could include comparing myself to others, belief in being unworthy and fear of rejection. You can reclaim your confidence. A Psychotherapist friend of mine says, "Name the fear and face it. Stand up to the bully." In the case of anxiety, the bully is part of our thought pattern.

A reasonable fear is about something real and happening in the present moment. If I encounter a dangerous animal, there is fear. Stress chemicals adrenaline and cortisol are released into the blood stream allowing for a quick motion towards safety. Reasonable fear is designed to protect us from present danger. Once clear of the threat, intensity of emotion will dissipate within a short time.

Anxiety is complex and quite different to standard fear. I could be very worried about encountering a snake in the future, even though there is no threat now. I might criticise myself for thinking this way and then ruminate on the issue for days on end. Anxiety is about issues not existing in the present moment and includes self-judgement.

Combine worry, false beliefs, imagined danger and harsh judgement and you have a good outline of what anxiety is. I could be resting comfortably at home and my thoughts drift to a mistake I made in the past. I feel panicky and sweaty judging myself. This an anxious response. This is what we will correct during our time together.

Another component of 'anxiety' is the effect on self-esteem. Anxiety says we are not enough, even when doing our best. It worries that bad things will happen. Anxiety says that we could get rejected by people we care about even if we are loved just fine by family and friends. On the whole anxiety is unfair because it restricts the expression of our best life.

An Anxiety Experience: "Well, it's what keeps me at home where there are no people. It is the post-mortem in my head after any encounters with people and the crippling shame and regret that follows. Anxiety has me waking during the night to a panic attack with no one there to comfort or reassure. Worrying that I am going to die because I cannot breathe, cannot catch my breath."

Together we will discuss how to heal anxiety without fear of catastrophe. In the early stages I suggest allowing physical anxious sensations 'to just be' without resistance. Rather than resisting feelings of anxiety, we'll focus together on building confidence and self-acceptance, in the present moment. Healing thoughts will be an important shift away from fighting anxiety.

Self-acceptance is allowing yourself to be as you are, and this, shortens anxiety.

When fear and self-judgement are no longer your primary focus, all that remains are physical symptoms of anxiety, which we will cover. This book sets out to help you get confidence and peace of mind back. What is brought into light can be healed. With mindfulness you can reduce and eliminate anxious symptoms.

ANXIETY CATEGORIES

Let's get more specific about what anxiety is. What we name, can be faced and worked through. Describing the types of anxiety is not for purposes of judgement. It is important to be aware of our thought patterns, in order to change them. (With this knowledge you can incorporate specific mindset tools for that anxiety type). Each person's anxiety will fit within at least 1 of 3 categories.

1) Fear of a Negative Outcome

The mind fears that something bad will happen. This can range from fear of discomfort to catastrophe and everything in between. Anxiety imagines a difficult event where mistake, pain, stress, setback, failure, illness or death will occur. The catastrophising beliefs are: Things are terrible. It will never be okay. Things will not work out.

Persistent fear of the negative, is anxiety. It is exaggerated and repeated in the mind, in a way that is not reasonable. This type of anxiety can include a belief that one's actions and inactions will cause further negative consequences, leaving one trapped and indecisive.

2) Fear of Not Being Enough

The mind fears being judged wrong and unworthy. Not being smart enough, strong, interesting, accomplished, popular, attractive, normal enough or some other variant of 'not enough.' We fear being considered unacceptable for all or part of who we are. The corresponding beliefs are: Other's are better, whilst oneself is inferior and embarrassed.

Comparing ourselves to someone else cannot lead to a healthy self-image. It's too focused on others criteria. This person will benefit from self-praise and self-acceptance. The subconscious mind takes on thoughts as truth whether they are mean or kind. In order to feel better, start speaking favourably about yourself. Acknowledge that all of you is enough, in this present moment.

3) Fear of Loss

The mind fears separation from someone or something valuable. Loss occurs in many forms. Passing of family, divorce, exclusion from a group and abandonment, are all associated with grief. Both adults and children struggle with this. The corresponding beliefs are: Blaming oneself, loss without gain and rejection without blessings.

Fear of separation is not limited to people. A loss of job, house, reputation, health, mental abilities and money are common. During the first 2 years of Covid-19 we were unable to visit family and move about freely. Collectively we lost a certain amount freedom and had to adapt. We fear loss from that which is familiar and valuable.

CHARACTERISTICS OF ANXIETY

- Imagination about the unknown
- High nervousness in specific situations
- Obsessiveness about others safety
- Worry about what others might be thinking
- Overextended trying to be good/perfect/selfless
- Imagining being judged wrong and not enough
- A fear of being rejected and alone
- Difficulty making decisions
- Ruminating on thoughts, particularly mistakes from the past
- Imagining the worst (pessimistic) with no evidence to back it up
- Binging on food, alcohol and cigarettes to avoid unwanted feelings
- OCD, nail biting, picking and compulsions to avoid unwanted feelings

CAN ANXIETY BE ABOUT THE PAST?

Yes it can. Ruminating on the past and ongoing guilt, is anxiety. An example of this is judging oneself for a mistake. Why did I say that? How could I do that? What's wrong with me? I once commented that a friend's hair "didn't look that bad." Indicating that my other friend had judged her hair bad but I thought it was okay. I feared their friendship might be at risk now.

My foot in the mouth moment gave me a tense chest. Years afterwards thinking about it still gave me the same tension. I was sweaty and embarrassed to think about it long after the event. To occasionally revisit a difficult memory is reasonable but to be fixated on the past, unable to let go of mistakes will require a healing intervention.

IF ONLY

We think, one day I will be acceptable. I would be, if only my parents loved me right. I'll have confidence, if only I am rich enough. I'll be approved of, if only I have a respectable career. I'll be complete, if only I am married or re-married. As a parent, I will have confidence if only my kids are healthy, smart and well-adjusted. And if only I had a toned, smooth and Instagram-able body.

'If only' is an anxious thought pattern.

Confidence is not attained by waiting for all goals to be achieved. Believing confidence and self-acceptance will come by meeting criteria in the future, is unfortunately not empowering us. A healthy, loving opinion of ourselves is available now. It is only achieved in the present moment.

The things you have tried to change, desires you have attempted to get rid of and suppressed emotions have caused anxiety. Freedom is not about getting rid of or changing any part of you. Anxious people have been trying to change who they are, for much of their life. Being integrated is about accepting and expressing more of you.

It is time to get present with self-acceptance. Lay down the weapons you have turned on yourself, including unfair beliefs of being not enough. Confidence need not be reliant on perfection but accepting the reality of who you are now. Take some time to be grateful for your value and achievements.

FIGHTING TO FEEL GOOD

Fighting oneself is exhausting. It can become a habit. You have used a tremendous amount of mental energy resisting anxiety. This need not go to waste. We are going to put that energy towards something useful. BEING, ACTING and THINKING in a way that is already aligned with healing.

Anxiety is part of the human experience and you need not go to war with it. Your conscious mind and subconscious mind are divided, when at war. There is a decision that needs to be made. It is this... I am willing to heal myself, instead of fighting myself.

You have a role in escalating or de-escalating the anxiety response. Better to lay down all those weapons and be true to yourself. Let go of guilt, self-defeating thoughts and accept the parts of you, judged wrong and bad for so long. This is part of the healing process.

You can be at peace. Or you can be at war. You cannot be both.

SELF-ACCEPTANCE AS A METHOD OF HEALING

Challenging anxiety with self-acceptance means shifting your being. It's not a strategy or tool. It is a change of mission for your subconscious mind. It is a new operating system for your 'inner computer.'

"My intentions, beliefs, thoughts and actions are aligned with healing. What I think and do, are part of the overarching mission to be at peace. Old ways of doubting, avoiding and fighting myself are done. I believe it is possible to heal. I am present. My mind is focused on the mission of self-love and self-acceptance. My thoughts are attracted to truth and empowerment. I take action on my highest thoughts. I release ways of being that no longer serve."

Spend more time every day focusing on thoughts and feelings you want to have. Over time your new, empowered thoughts will become habit and this will become what you experience in life.

HIGH ALERT

Anxiety is a protection mechanism against negative outcomes and judgement. What if it all goes wrong and I fail? What if people see my weakness? The problem with anxiety is that we are on high alert far too often. Anxiety is mostly a waste of imagination, fearing possible outcomes that rarely eventuate.

I lived my life on high alert. I feared most emotions, including what they revealed. Positive emotions show people who I am, which brings too much attention my way. Negative ones show weakness. I tried to hide them all, avoiding being seen as weird and too intense.

I was ready to defend myself, deflect responsibility and play dumb. When feeling under threat, during adolescence and early adult life, I manipulated people. I didn't want to get into trouble and have my parents think less of me. Rarely relaxed, even with friends, my 'are they looking at me radar,' warned of potential psychological danger.

Any of these headlines could have been applied to my personality. "Smart but lacks confidence", "Scared to be seen", "Overly sensitive" or "Calm but quick to anger." I worked hard to control what people thought about me. I lied unnecessarily, which became an avoidance habit. Some believed I was calm however this was a façade because generally I was nervous.

Much energy was spent on image preservation, which detracted from genuine connection. Controlling others takes away from the present moment. I was too worried about being judged as **bad**, seen as **not enough** and finally **rejected**.

I thought, when someone disapproves of my fake self, it doesn't matter, but if someone rejects and abandons the real me, that's devastating. It seems devastating but is it really? Is too much importance placed on what a small group of people think? How likely is it that manipulating will create fulfilling relationships? Can authenticity reduce the anxious response?

It may be that there is too much emphasis on presenting a desirable image of oneself. This less than real version of ourselves takes a huge amount of energy to manage. A fake image is maintained with controlled body language, calculated lies, suppressed emotions and trying to read someone's mind so as to deliver a confident reply.

Every mask is a self-portrait. Beneath mine was a skinny guy with little self-esteem. How could I have acquired healthy self-esteem? Growing up, there were no role models or mentors leading the way in empowerment. Knowledge for managing emotions and mindset was rarely spoken about. I'm not blaming, that's just the way it was.

When naughty, I did enough good to slip under the radar and I knew when to apologise so people would leave me alone. Being dishonest was easy. The best guidance I received was to work for what I want in life. I possessed an entrepreneurial spirit from a young age. I began working at 8 years old and created several businesses from ages 12-20.

- I started a lawnmowing service. Mowing my parent's lawn was expected but I could get paid from the neighbours
- I created a photography business, designed calendars and won awards for my local nature shots
- My herb business offered medicinal teas and legal highs which I sold at markets while working 2 part time jobs

At an interview for my first job I answered a questionnaire. It asked that I rate my work ethic and attributes out of 10. I scored myself honestly with 6s, 7s and 8s and didn't get a call back. I then applied at the store next door with 9s and 10s and was immediately hired. Nowadays I gladly score myself highly with the intention of following through on that promise.

I wanted people to think I was the best, while appearing to do it easily. "Wow look at how much he's accomplished. How did he even do that?" Sometimes they would say it too, which my ego loved. I wanted to appear interesting and special whilst applying the least amount of effort.

Here is what my competitive mind wanted to believe. "I am effortlessly the best." I overcompensated for feeling less than enough. My peers were more charming to the opposite sex, socially capable, fitter and stronger. I decided I'd be the smartest and fastest, however that did not create a healthy self-esteem as the goal was still seeking validation from others.

It is worth being conscious of the difference between self-acceptance and receiving it from others.

Self-acceptance is independent of mistakes and successes. It does not rely on a comparison of someone who has failed worse than you, in order to feel better. It is a present-moment recognition that who you are is okay. There is the realisation of truth as your heart softens and mind becomes clear. It is an enlightened moment.

SOCIAL ANXIETY

Despite social anxiety I revelled at large gatherings where I could blend into the crowd. In a sea of people, it was easy to have fun and get wild. Intense activities of sport, reef diving and partying with drugs gave this introvert enough stimulation and cover, to bypass a low self-esteem.

Drugs worked and they didn't. Hours of total confidence and heightened energy led to fun and euphoric experiences but underneath it all was no self-development. Do I have more belief in myself? Am I adding value to the world at large? Have I done the work to love challenging parts of myself?

Small social gatherings were the hardest to navigate. At cafés there was just nowhere to hide, uncomfortable sitting still and fearing being the centre of attention. How do I even order at this café, is it counter or table service? I worried about being seen 'worrying' and people thinking I'm weird.

SOCIAL VICTORY

A favourite social success involved setting aside fear and expressing myself. When single I signed up for Cuban Salsa dance lessons. This situation meant putting my uncoordinated body on full display in a well-lit room, fully sober and asking it to move with rhythm. Think, 'Big Bang Theory's' awkward character of Sheldon Cooper on the dancefloor.

I arrived early as a class was finishing up, so I hid in the bathroom for a few minutes. An anxious predicament. Did I want to be early or late? Neither are ideal. I decided it was better to be slightly early, so I didn't miss any instructions. The dance space was large, with wooden floors. It had high ceilings and windows from top to bottom, allowing natural light to fill the room and a 3rd story view of the city.

I entered the room with the first class still going. 45 dancers, all women, moved to the high energy beats. In my mind they were coordinated, fit and pumping to the music. This amount of feminine energy is exciting and initiates any man to step up energetically. I walked as tall as I could down the length of the room towards the only seating, which was front on to all the dancers.

I was nervous watching them at first and didn't want to be a distraction or have them think I was being rude. I instead, focused on holding an energetic space for things to be as they are. I didn't have to be or do anything. I am neither good nor bad. My presence would simply be what it is, I felt my body relax.

My class had a mix of both men and women who were younger and older than I. We were taught basic moves and I found myself to be an absolute novice. I was slow to learn but learn I did. We progressed onto partnered dancing and it was fun. I stayed for 5 weekly classes and then moved on.

To get there at all was a victory because I told anxiety to get stuffed! I challenged fear with action and nothing bad happened. Nerves are part of the body's warning system that perceives something as risky. I have often used my confidence to dance, as a measure of how strong I am against social anxiety. It is okay for the body to be seen. Okay to be uncoordinated and just fine to express joy.

DRIVING ME CRAZY

From 2007 until 2009 I worked as a Bus Driver, in Airlie Beach QLD. It was a time of transformation and spiritual awakening in my life. I had issues with chronic fatigue and anxiety, which were to burden me for several more years.

I neared the end of my shift one night, with just 1 passenger on board. An older gentleman was seated at the back of the bus. It was 10:00pm and there were 5 stops left. I made a simple driving error, oversteering at a roundabout and needed to correct the vehicle. No damage was caused but I was clumsy and the man noticed. He seemed fixated on me, like a hawk preparing its strike.

I was anxious in the pit of my stomach and sweated. I felt embarrassed about the simple mistake and could sense judgement from the passenger. I was in my early twenties and imagined the man had vast experience in driving compared to me. I made my last stops and knew I would face him.

After what felt like an hour (it was 10 minutes), we arrived. I opened the front door ready to accept condemnation from the passenger as he disembarked. Several seconds passed, I heard no judgement or footsteps. I looked over my left shoulder and no one was there. I hadn't opened the back door, (nor had I picked up or dropped off anyone else since the roundabout) so where was he?

Either the man had teleported out of a moving vehicle, like a scene from Star Trek or there never was anyone there to begin with. No one was on the bus.

Judgement was there, as was the anxiety. My beliefs created the hallucination; an imaginary character in my mind to point out I'm not good enough. "The mistake was terrible, I'm a bad driver, I'm not enough, this person is better than me. I would receive condemnation and be proven unworthy."

Many people make mistakes driving. For someone living life on high alert, panic can set in, especially if the error was seen by others. Anxiety said it was not okay to make mistakes, and even created an imaginary father figure, as a higher authority to make the point.

A reasonable mind would say it is understandable to make an error while I am still learning. When doing something new, no one is 100% capable. A healthy self-esteem says, I'm not confident at this task, yet I will be with practise. I will continue to learn. I am perfectly imperfect.

MADE UP THOUGHTS

Put simply, the mind assigns meaning to events. Born from this are false and incomplete beliefs, like I'm a bad driver. Anxiety takes imagination to incredible levels. The made up beliefs which are untrue, also spawn more disempowering beliefs. I am a bad driver, leads to I must be not enough, which can lead to I will be rejected and alone.

Understanding that beliefs are made up means we have the ability to change them. They have no power. They were formed unconsciously (not on purpose). By recognising that, being an occasional bad driver is okay and does not equal rejection.

When you notice a belief that is made up, I suggest you question it. Hold that belief up to the light of truth and it's power will be found non-existent. Where did this belief originate? What is definitely true about me? What are my terrific qualities? Does the meaning assigned to this situation make sense?

These questions will erode the foundations of limiting beliefs, causing them to crumble. Be firm with your mind when challenging and changing your beliefs. Don't allow one disempowering thought to continue, unchecked by the spotlight of truth.

AUTHENTIC SELF

We now know that thoughts of doom and catastrophe are made up. Imaginations that you are not worthy are likewise false. They are just thoughts your mind is stuck thinking, on repeat. Wouldn't it be freeing to let go of self-judgement and share your truth with others?

It can be very peaceful being yourself. There is no exhaustion trying to maintain an illusion, that you think people want to see. Once you reveal yourself to the world, there will be no fear of people discovering secrets about you – because they already know. Successes, failures, strengths and limitations can be freely revealed.

I can tell you that there is no one in my life that I wish to see less of their real self. Honest thoughts and raw feelings are expressions of an authentic persona. To express authenticity activates the heart of self and all those who bear witness.

It's one of the most special and vulnerable parts of relationships. Knowing somebody deeply and saying, "I see you. I accept you." The heart will open after what was kept deep inside is finally expressed.

REALISTIC MIND

Your language reveals your beliefs. A therapist is trained to notice such patterns that are extreme and could be troubling you. They listen for beliefs that might be causing emotional disturbances and ask questions to help you find a missing piece of your puzzle.

How can it be known that beliefs cause emotional disturbances?

If a person believes the worst will **always happen** based on **no evidence**, this is anxiety. Their perception is **neither realistic** nor are the events even **occurring** at all. If worries are constantly distressing you, this is anxiety.

You can train your mind to let go of unhelpful, limiting beliefs. We'll do it together.

Thoughts that are extreme tend to replay in the mind **until corrected**. Think about 'thoughts' in terms of, the truer they are the quieter they will be. If you are ever wondering what needs healing, start correcting the loudest and most intrusive thoughts.

When you have a healing thought, it doesn't need to last a long time. A moment of healing is exactly that, a moment. After this moment, there is stillness. The ah ha realisation fully clears the mess of thoughts that occupy space in our mind.

You might realise the truth and accept it. What was difficult for a long time is now complete. The truth is complete (not riddled with delusion). We don't re-hash **true thoughts** hundreds of times. There is an opening of the mind and heart, through truth, acceptance, gratitude or forgiveness.

> *"True thoughts heal the mind, like medicine heals and ailment."*

Are some of my thoughts highly unrealistic? Is anxiety addictive because we seek results from a delusion that can never be fulfilled? Do you have loud thoughts that replay many times? Could it be that healing is needed?

The term extreme thinking is in reference to beliefs that don't match reality. The beliefs are incomplete, taking a strong position to one extreme. You don't need to change your authentic self, just connect with it. The suggestion here is to align your beliefs with the reality of who you are and how life works. This is a sign of self-mastery. Having very little delusion in the mind.

The opposite of delusional anxiety is delusional optimism and high self-esteem, far exceeding reality. I don't recommend extreme positivity for the same reason I don't recommend negativity, it is not truth. The healing approach is the middle ground, balanced, authentic and true thinking.

> *Your therapist's goal for you should be awareness of self, realistic expectations and balanced thoughts. There is very little instance of anxiety and addiction in those focused on truth.*

STRESS AND ANXIETY

Going for a run, stresses my body. If my leg cramps in the present moment, that is stress. The 'thought' of running however causes no strain. Visualising my shoes hitting the footpath causes no stress nor does it make me sweat.

Sitting at home thinking negatively about running or feeling guilty for not exercising, is anxiety. Anxiety is thinking of something that is not happening here and now. Anxiety is about **somewhere** you are not and **some time** you are not.

If at 3 weeks before a dentist appointment I am worried about pain, this is anxiety. Fear of pain, in the waiting room before the procedure, is anxiety. When there *is* pain, that's stress in the present moment.

If I'm guilt-ridden about financial decisions, this is anxiety. If I am worried there might never be enough money to pay the bills, this is anxiety. When I am unable to pay a bill in the present moment, this is stress.

If I'm afraid of arguing with my wife, that's anxiety. When I walk through the front door worried what sort of mood she's in, that is anxiety. When there is actual raised voices, this is stress in the present moment.

HEALING ANXIETY

LOUISE'S WORRY

I consulted with Louise who worried about her daughter Charlotte, travelling to Cambodia. She worried for about 2 hours every day. There was risk to the trip but reasonably safe, like other countries in the region.

Louise believed that discussing dangers of travel, would make her daughter prepared and safe. Charlotte was dismissive of concerns, preferring to be positive and excited. The more optimistic her daughter's attitude, the more worried Louise became.

Where was Louise's mind in location? Cambodia. When was her mind in time? 2 months into the future. What was she imagining? A bad outcome. It's not bad or wrong, it's just an anxiety pattern.

Worry is a non-present and pessimistic form of caring.

Me: "When you become present, you will stop worrying. A small shift in approach can make a vast difference. You can bring your mind-focus back to here and now." I asked Louise questions to get more information and enable awareness.

Me: "Where does your daughter live?"

Louise: "We live together, we keep arguing and I try to warn her of possible dangers."

Me: "Will she be travelling alone or with people?"

Louise: "With a friend and they will both volunteer at an orphanage."

Me: "Have you met her friend and researched the orphanage online?"

Louise: "Oh yes, I've known her friend for years and the orphanage looks pretty good. I guess I just don't want her to get hurt."

Me: "Have you travelled? Were there difficult times and also special moments you experienced?"

Louise: "I have travelled many times. Yes, there were both."

Me: "Are you going to miss Charlotte?"

Louise: "Yes, terribly."

Me: "There may be risks but she will also have good times. For the next 2 months you will see your daughter at home. It would be terrible (using your words) to miss connecting in the present. You are missing out on connecting with her now due to this worry. You want her ready for potential dangers because you care. Your worrying, is care, that hasn't been received."

Me: "You can earn her receptivity by balancing the conversation."

Louise: "What do you mean?"

Me: "When both of you are relaxed, tell her of your overseas travel stories. Start with the good times. What you love about culture, food and even a gentleman you may have met. Once feeling connected with Charlotte, share what went wrong and what you learnt. Think of it as having a conversation with someone you trust.

Pause to let her ask questions. Don't rush the conversation either… No doubt she wants to be safe on her journey but also enthusiastic. Give her a little of both. Excitement for the journey ahead and maybe the top 1-2 dangers to be aware of. A balance of good and bad is easier to hear, than all negative."

Louise: "Wow I never thought of it that way."

Louise: "Also, now that I think about it, she already is well prepared, smart and trustworthy. My worry had just taken over."

Me: "Great, share that with her too. Hey, I have been overly worried, it just means I care and love you. I travelled when a little older than you and overall it was a fantastic experience."

We went deeper. With this next question, we explore what would happen if the opposite were true. How many downsides would there be if she didn't go to Cambodia? What would Charlotte miss?

- Cultural experiences
- Expanding her mind
- Making friends
- New food experiences

- Helping the children
- Growing spiritually
- Memories for a lifetime
- She would lose her biggest dream

Me: "What if she missed out on all that?"

Louise: "Yes, it would be terrible. I still really want her to go."

Me: "So your smart, well-prepared daughter, whom you trust, is having the time of her life in South Asia. She will have an amazing time and face a challenge or two. There will be both and she'll grow as a person. How excited are you for her to have this experience?"

Louise: "I'm over the moon for her!"

Me: "It sounds like you are now getting excited for her to go travelling. What are the benefits to you supporting her?"

Louise: "A peaceful home. Enthusiasm. A loving connection for the next 2 months before she leaves."

Me: "Why don't you go home and share these things with her from the heart."

Both of us are beaming in the clinic now, knowing the open-hearted conversation that will take place between them. Louise can be caring in the present moment, sharing excitement and pearls of wisdom. She can still get her point across. Charlotte will likely be receptive when offered a true, balanced perspective.

Me: "Any anxiety about her trip?"

Louise: "Only a little now, I am more excited. I had been focusing totally on the negative. I couldn't see the positive and bigger picture. I can focus on connecting in the present moment."

Worrying over children's safety is a big cause of anxiety. We hope they are going to make good choices and generally lead a happy life. Anxiety arises because they will be exposed to difficult experiences that we can't control and shield them from.

There is an effective and beautiful way to not worry about family. It is, to be excited for them. Once we see that the intention for worrying is **showing care** for people, we can display it purposefully. Does challenge enable kids to grow new skills? Have you found the hidden excitement in your anxiety? Could you demonstrate worry in a balanced way?

Children will go through unique challenges and this will shape their personality. Rather than attempting to shield children from life, it may be more effective to guide them with a realistic perspective. There will be wonderful times as well as challenges to prepare for.

Don't worry if you aren't sure exactly what to share with your kids now. Start by having one balanced conversation with a beloved family member. Include themes that are both optimistic and pessimistic. Notice the difference in how your communication is received.

ADAM'S STORY

I shared the above insights with a client Adam. He has a significant role in a food production company, overseeing logistics, ordering and operations. Prior to visiting my office he would go several weeks binging on alcohol, then several weeks sober. This pattern persisted for two decades and caused major problems in all areas of his life.

Adam successfully quit drinking with hypnotherapy (10 months clear at time of writing) yet had substantial anxiety about work. There was excessive worry about what could go wrong. He was a problem solver and kept the operation on track. Solving work problems was a skill but at home, could not stop. Worry was intrusive on weekends and late at night.

On a recent Saturday, relaxing at home, he created 6 solutions for something that didn't even need fixing. Such was the extent of his mind not switching off. Adam asked me with genuine interest, "Why do I worry so much?"

I allowed my own mind to consider an answer for a few seconds and shared with him the difference between stress and anxiety. "Stress exists always in the present moment. For example, if there is workplace conflict, that *is* stress. If worried about *possible* conflict, that's anxiety. Anxiety is never in a present time or present location."

HEALING ANXIETY

Me: "In your role of food production, anxiety would be worrying stock might not turn up. It's one possible outcome your mind is stuck on. You can't fix this problem because there *is* no problem. There is no issue with the delivery, only the possibility of a problem.

Now, if stock does not arrive, that's stress. It is a present moment issue, which you can solve. Something 'is' wrong, not something 'could' go wrong. If stock doesn't turn up, you take action, don't you? Arrange a replacement delivery or check which stores nearby can transfer stock etc.

If worried about stock not turning up, I suggest checking one time that the order was sent. When a job has been done correctly, and you check once, then train your mind to **let go**. Say, "I'm done. It's complete. I'm moving on." Use this in any situation your mind tends to be on high alert for.

If there is no action to take, then it is not useful to worry, it's just a habit. While you are thinking more reasonably, anxious feelings will lessen. Train your mind to move on by getting back to your tasks or do something positive like having a glass of fresh water. This shifts your focus, has health benefits and no downsides."

Anxiety thinks hard on 'maybe' going to happen.

He wrote an insight on his notepad while I talked. Worry is never about here and now.

Adam: "There is a factory being built at work. It is a big project. There are delays and communication problems between management and tradespeople. My mind thinks about that factory every day. My mind is 5 months in the future and 20km away."

Me: "Yes, that is anxiety. One thing to remember. Worry means you care. It has some legitimacy. Each day ask this one question, is there any action needed now to enable the factory build to continue smoothly?"

Adam: "Today I just need to email Bob. That will take 5 minutes.

In a few days there is a weekly meeting with the key players."

Me: "Great, do your due diligence. Send the email and spend 20 minutes jotting notes to prepare for the meeting. Total time doing what's needed is 25 minutes, then you must move on."

Like Louise, he worries, which is ungrounded caring. Adam cares about the company. They stuck by him, even during alcoholism. It makes sense he wants to do an excellent job. I encouraged him to do his work mindfully and to also enjoy family time on weekends.

Adam: "It's like I need permission to switch off. My immediate manager, the CEO and my wife actually tell me not to work late at night or on weekends. They ask that I stop replying to emails."

Me: "Great, you have just touched on the law of feedback. Those in your environment recognise your quality work. They don't need you to do any more. Your partner, boss and CEO ask you to slow down. Your own mind indicates wisdom in slowing down. You will benefit greatly from the ability to switch off when you choose to."

Me: "Maybe you just care a lot about work or are used to having an active mind. Caring is appropriate and you can, in mindful doses. Draw a line in the sand when you are done worrying." I pause for several seconds.

Me: "Do you think you used to binge hard on alcohol to switch off your mind?"

Adam: "Absolutely." Again, we pause for several seconds to draw attention to the present.

Me: "Previously you had avoided dealing with anxiety. You drank for weeks at a time which gave you a break from the constant mind activity. Now, you are dealing with your problem. Well done. You did not give up. You are facing uncomfortable feelings and are currently in the healing process, learning to self-regulate.

Adam was deep in thought. He had at least 2 lessons to think about. The first was that worry is about problems that don't exist, only things that could happen. The second was that uncomfortable feelings mean he is engaging in the healing process.

FOUNDATIONS OF MASTERING ANXIETY

Knowledge
Gaining information contributes to confidence. With understanding we are empowered to make better decisions and control our destiny. Without knowledge, anxiety fills in the unknown with doubts, worries and imagination.

Taking Action
Finishing tasks give feelings of accomplishment in the present. We don't have to 'think about things' that are complete. Quality actions made with knowledge, is wisdom. Procrastination and avoiding responsibility are anxious responses.

Asking for Support
By getting help, you are expressing that anxiety is occurring and it is your mission to heal. Anxiety keeps us hidden away, missing an opportunity for healing. Getting support from a person you are safe and comfortable with, is an act of reclaiming power.

Intention Setting
Setting an intention each day gives direction to your subconscious mind. In doing so you are influencing your frame of mind. For example, my mission is to be present. If the mind drifts off to the past or future, then my intention re-focuses me on here and now.

A Sense of Safety
Being safe must be the number one priority. At home and work, feeling unsafe is a major cause of anxiety. Having been through trauma, the mind will build a wall to keep out perceived dangers, both real and imagined. Be safe and look after one another.

A Sense of Fair

Being selfish misses caring for other's needs. Being selfless misses looking after oneself. Fairness is love, where all are taken care of (including you). A fair person recognises the value of others and themselves. Both giving and receiving are part of healthy interactions.

Mindfulness

The quality of breathing, self-talk and general mental health can fall under mindful attention. Awareness of thought patterns that are useful vs not useful, is a sign of mastery. I encourage mindful attention of your thoughts, beliefs and nervous system.

Reducing Overwhelm

A life full of stress means we have taken on too much. The nervous system is frazzled and overwhelmed. Creating a balanced lifestyle with space to think, rest and enjoy ourselves is important. When more relaxed in general we tend to sleep better too.

Quality Sleep

Safety, mindfulness techniques and reducing anxiety help improve sleep. Making rest a priority is imperative. Small changes really can make a great difference to sleep quality. With proper rest we are more likely to improve mood, energy and mental clarity.

Self-acceptance

An integrated person accepts all that is unique about themselves, including: strengths, abilities, personality traits and desires. This also means accepting limitations, mistakes, weaknesses and shadow side.

Social Confidence

Being comfortable with socialising, dating and job interviews allows us more opportunities and expression. We all want to feel at ease, so we can enjoy the best things in life. Social confidence means self-acceptance and much less worry about what others *might* be thinking about us.

Creating a Balanced Mind and Life

It is time to 'get real' about: mental health, physical health, marriage, money, sex, family, food, travel, exercise, career and self-esteem. No situation is all good, there are challenges. No situation is all bad, there are blessings. Expectations outside of reality, are fantasies and nightmares that make us anxious.

Reality

If your mind is believing that imagination is reality, you've got an anxious pest living upstairs. Double check that your thoughts are as factual as possible. Ask several times each day, "What is definitely true in this situation?" Do your best to stop focusing on the unknown and imagination. Keep tuning into truth.

Alignment

When relationships, work environment and lifestyle are right for you, confidence is higher. When aligned there is less anxiety. Picture a relationship where both partners agree on their financial plan and follow-through. Imagine a workplace with fair pay and the job is rewarding. These are examples of alignment.

SELF-ESTEEM

How you regard yourself is an important aspect of mental health. It relates to belief in capabilities, and how you value yourself. An accurate (or healthy) self-opinion is neither too low nor high. A healthy self-esteem is actually in the middle, regarding oneself in alignment with reality.

A healthy self-esteem recognises what it is to be a human being. There are strengths and weaknesses, capabilities and limitations, ups and downs, successes and failures and these are fundamentally acceptable and unavoidable.

"Self-esteem is not the euphoria or buoyancy that may temporarily be induced by a drug, compliment or love affair. It is not an illusion or hallucination. If it is not grounded in reality, if it is not built over time through the appropriate operation of mind, it is not self-esteem." Says Psychotherapist Nathaniel Branden

An inaccurate self-esteem can go 1 of 2 ways, above or below what is real.

HIGH SELF-ESTEEM

Those with an exaggerated self-opinion have inflated beliefs of themselves. This can be observed as arrogant, superior, righteous and selfish. With a high self-esteem, the person is less likely to acknowledge their flaws. Much energy is used to maintain a false self-image.

A high self-esteem person shows their better qualities and blames others when things go wrong. They miss chances to improve because they are already wonderful, according to their own perception. The higher self-esteem person worries less about other viewpoints, often regarding their behaviour correct. They are likely to take criticism as a threat and express anger outwardly.

Popular teachings say that 'high self-esteem' is a good thing. We are addicted to getting high as a society. The risk of an exaggerated opinion of oneself, is being anxious to maintain this fantastic, yet unreal image.

It's like a Christmas lunch that is excessive. Too much and one becomes over inflated and full of gas. It looked good on appearance but you wish you had less. The high self-esteem goal sounds appealing, because it is the opposite of low self-esteem. This does not make it a valid goal. Getting high on something extreme or delusional, is problematic.

LOW SELF-ESTEEM

A low self-opinion occurs when one regards themselves less than they are. They often place their needs last when part of a group. This can be observed as people pleasing and selflessness. The low self-esteem person believes they should be a good and kind person. They avoid setting goals that could upset people, yet a thought nags their mind. "I deserve better than this."

With a low self-esteem the person denies their great qualities and rarely takes credit for success. The lower self-esteem person fears letting people down. They take criticism as a failure and more often express anger inwardly. Sticking with the Christmas theme, low self-esteem would manifest as the over-giver who doesn't eat or eats last. They would be fussing over everybody else, making sure all are taken care of.

It seems natural for the lower self-esteem person to serve. They regard others needs as important and often forgo their desires, in order to look after everybody else. This person will need convincing that they are in fact valuable. It is okay to rest, without feeling guilty. It okay to simply please yourself.

- Neither a high or low self-esteem is bad nor wrong, it is just too much, if your goal is balance
- The closer your self-esteem is with reality the healthier it is
- A higher self-esteem person takes care of themselves more often
- A lower self-esteem person takes care of others more often

"When our self-esteem is moderate/realistic, we are less vulnerable to anxiety; we release less cortisol into our bloodstream when under stress, and it is less likely to linger in our system." Says Psychologist Guy Winch.

HEALTHY SELF-ESTEEM

With a healthy self-esteem you regard yourself exactly as you are. An accurate description of self is preferred, over exaggerated delusions. A healthy self-esteem is observed as fair, caring, truthful, responsible and balancing the needs of self with others. A win-win outcome is preferred whenever possible.

With a healthy self-esteem there is little anxiety about being better or worse than others. You are not acting superior nor inferior. A moderate, true self opinion is grounded in reality. (It's like a Christmas lunch you enjoyed in moderation). There is no attachment to a false or future version of self.

A 'healthy self-esteem' is balanced between high and low. It is grounded in reality and the present moment. Those with a healthy self-esteem acknowledge strengths and limitations, successes and failures, and accept themselves.

I want us to focus in on the word opinion, in the phrase "self-esteem is the opinion of oneself." We all have a sense of who we are, based on opinions. Unfair praise and criticism can skew a true sense of self. At times, I have been called terrible when doing my best. I have also been labelled wonderful when I didn't even try.

These are opinions that are not only, not based in fact, but don't take into account the whole person's character. Opinions themselves differ depending on who is delivering them. So why do we place importance on extreme and varied labels? How do we realise a healthy self-esteem?

Comments that are extremely good or bad don't serve any purpose but to deliver a temporary lift or dip in self-esteem. Neither compliments nor criticism have anything to do with developing your healthy self image.

An off the cuff criticism is labelling just a tiny fraction of the whole person. Likewise feeling euphoric when gaining the attention of a new lover is not a solution for self-esteem. A healthy self-esteem is less concerned with extreme viewpoints, preferring reality.

There is only one truth of who you are as a person. It is simply this. You are who you are. Free from stories, labels, anxieties and memories that have been given too much importance in the grand scheme of things. You are all of you. No more, no less.

I am what I am.

I have an exercise for you. I would like you to take control of the narrative about yourself. Your thoughts have power and everyone has certain thoughts that can be improved. Notice positive (perfect) thoughts or negative (terrible) thoughts about self, and correct them with realistic descriptions.

REALITY-BASED THINKING EXERCISE

This process is an opportunity to take control of your thinking. For the next 7 days, be mindful of your self-talk. Note the words used to describe yourself, that are inaccurate and exaggerated. A self-evaluation based in fact, guards against slipping too low or high in esteem. You will think balanced and therefore start to feel balanced.

Example 1) "My partner is angry, that means they hate me. I screwed up. It's too hard. I must be hard to love."

Change it to reality-based thinking.

"My partner is venting frustration. This is a chance to listen and provide care. It is likely a small aspect of my being that is frustrating them. I have an opportunity to gain understanding and can then make a decision that is fair. There have been hundreds of loving moments in this relationship and thousands in my lifetime. I am on the whole, a lovable person."

Example 2) "I have failed as usual. This is terrible and wrong. I must be hopeless. No wonder I can't succeed at anything."

Change it to reality-based thinking.

"These thoughts are very interesting. For a first attempt, my effort was good. With practice I will become more skilful, like I have with my many achievements. Mistakes are not points against my self-worth. I am okay with myself while I am learning to get it right. I am okay asking for help."

Example 3) "My new lover said they love me. I must be wonderful. I can do no wrong. We'll probably be peaceful and have great sex forever."

Change it to reality-based thinking.

"My partner said they love me. If we end up living together there will be a tremendous responsibility to another human being. It's important we are realistic in our expectations and communicate often. Truth and trust will become more important than sex. Euphoria is not a bonus to my self-esteem. There will be good times as well as challenges to face together."

Example 4) "Gosh I am so wonderful, handsome and successful every single time. I am just the best and perfect and did I mention how handsome and wonderful I am."

Again, change it to reality-based thinking.

"That's interesting, my self-opinion is very high. If I think I'm perfect, I could miss an opportunity to learn. I make mistakes most days. I have genuine qualities and some areas that can still be improved. Life is a team effort. I am grateful for the help others give me. I am humble to those who teach."

Will you take on this mission to accept the real you? Change your inner dialogue to reality-based and balanced thinking and you will heal your self-esteem. Include praise for self and acknowledge those that contributed to success. Challenge false thoughts by asking, "What is true about me?" and "Can I align my thoughts and actions with reality?"

ACKNOWLEDGING SELF AND OTHERS

Sportspeople demonstrate how to keep self-esteem in perspective. They are called "Legends," "Champions" or "Unbelievable Athletes." When giving interviews, players aim to reduce over-praise they receive from media.

Praise will be showered upon them. This is unbalanced, so they acknowledge teammates, luck, hard work, coaching staff, physiotherapists, parents, family, their partner and the crowd, for getting them the win. With a healthy self-esteem your capabilities are acknowledged, and so are the people that made success possible. It is real.

I could not have achieved anything substantial, if it were not for the knowledge and support from others. Many people have helped on my journey. The few that have made the biggest difference bring tears of gratitude to think about.

A healthy self-esteem is realistic, acknowledging the contribution of self and others. It warms the heart when expressed genuinely. Yes, I scored the winning goal AND hundreds of people contributed to the team. Yes, I did a great job AND it wouldn't have been possible without workmates who supported and challenged me to be better.

SUPPORT FROM THE PACK

Lionesses are considered by many to be magnificent hunters. Their size and power command attention but a lioness hunting alone, has only an 18% success rate. One of the great apex predators on the planet does not triumph every time. Only 1 out of every 5.5 solo efforts leads to a meal.

With support from the pride success is boosted to 30%. Using tall grass and darkness for cover, lionesses become even more effective. With specialised strategies success happens more often. The point here is not about judging these big cats however focusing on resources that make you better. Whether beast or human, support and launching into action works.

TRAFFIC LIGHTS

When driving, a person of high self-esteem will more likely speed to beat a red traffic light. When the light is orange I go, go, go. I am more likely to travel over the speed limit and break rules, because where I'm going, is more important than the law and road safety. Nothing will slow me down. I do what works for me.

The low self-esteem person will more likely brake suddenly, when the traffic light changes to orange. I am scared of doing the wrong thing and worried what other road users think of me. I stay in the slow lane on the motorway, allowing others to get where they are going. I am more likely to place the needs of the many, above personal needs.

Those with a healthy self-esteem balance self-importance, with that of everyone else. I change lanes because I need to, not in a submissive nor aggressive way. With a healthy self-esteem, the intention is responsibility and equality. I allow others to pass in front of me, when safe to do so. I drive with care and adhere to the road rules.

Self-esteem is not a mystical thing to grasp. It is revealed when you make a decision. Will it be for self, others or fairness for everybody?

RESPONSIBILITY AND ANXIETY

If I was driving 15km over the speed limit and got hit by a gentleman reversing out his driveway without looking, who should take responsibility? Both of us. I was irresponsible, travelling over the expected speed for that area, meaning less time for others to make safe decisions and corrections. The man was also reckless. His careless action contributed to the crash.

Responsibility can be assigned where it is appropriate. Random blame slinging is not useful however being aware of the causes that lead to a particular effect is. A healthy self-esteem wants truth and knowledge.

Being responsible does not mean doing everything. The point is to be effective. It is imprudent to take on so much, that you become burdened. Those with a healthy esteem look for opportunities to take 'appropriate responsibility' and encourage others to do the same.

Appropriate and responsibility are two of the most boring words anyone could put together in a sentence but stick with me, they can be used to dramatically reduce your anxiety. It can make a big difference to decide how much and whose burden, you take on.

DEBORAH'S STORY

Deborah was anxious about her young brother Ryan, who moved far away from home. He was making foolish financial decisions and accumulating debt. Deborah and her mum were worried about his future. I said, "If both of you are worried about Ryan's spending habits then he must be having quite a lot of excitement. What do you disapprove of?"

Deborah: "Motorbikes… and recently 2 dogs he can't afford to take care of. He spends on alcohol and parties a lot. When he crashed his car, our Mum replaced it. She keeps paying for his mistakes and bills, so I'm worried about her too."

Me: "From what you said, Ryan is having a great time driving fast vehicles, partying and when expenses get high, money is provided. There are no financial consequences. He has less concerns because you and your Mum have taken on more responsibility than appropriate.

Me: "Consider that from Ryan's point of view there are no consequences. Why would he worry?"

Deborah: "We tell him he needs to be more careful and says he'll do better next time. But doesn't change anything."

Me: "Ryan is currently hearing two opposing messages 1) Be financially responsible. 2) And if you are not responsible, money will be given whenever you need it. Anxiety is high because you have taken on Ryan's burden, rather than him dealing with consequences for his actions and you are worried about Mum, who is making a choice, to fund his mistakes too. It's not wrong, that's just the truth.

Taking away his financial worry, denies him the benefits of responsibility. Ryan growing into an adult might include some hard lessons, like excessive spending leads to debt. Then, choosing discipline to pay down what is owed. Ryan stepping up will mean changing his lifestyle. He knows it. You know it too."

Deborah: "That sounds about right."

It occurred to me to check if Deborah was being responsible or too care-free with her own goals.

Me: "One more thing. Sometimes when worried for others, we are less active solving our own problems. Is there any procrastination going on for you at the moment?" Bingo! The lightbulb switches on in her mind.

Deborah: "I have been avoiding my issues and drinking too much."

Me: "Any financial decisions you have been avoiding?"

Deborah: Nods her head.

These often appear together:

- Worried about others who don't want to take responsibility
- Taking on their burden and rescuing
- Avoiding dealing with one's own problems

HEALING ANXIETY

For all those with anxiety, focus on you first! Those who have taken care of themselves are far less anxious about other people's problems. If you have abundant time, money and energy for others, by all means give but when you are struggling, it is appropriate to look after yourself. Consider passing excess stress, back to the person who created it in the first place.

Reflect on whether you put off your tasks, by focusing on other people's problems.

PEOPLE PLEASING AND BOUNDARIES

Affirmation: "I stand up for myself and what is fair. I am important."

Giving beyond your physical and emotional limit is a sign of people pleasing. An example of this would be sacrificing recovery time, to solve other people's problems. Think about the boss or family member who has asked so much. You say, "yes," to make them happy, even though you are struggling.

Allowing boundaries to be crossed is anxiety related. At work, we say yes fearing possible loss of hours or getting fired. At home we over-give to avoid conflict with partner. Around friends, saying yes to something undesirable avoids rejecting someone.

Recall the relationships where you walked on eggshells trying to please yet were anxious of doing the wrong thing. It's no one's fault that giving so much became a habit. We never got told to make ourselves the priority. In fact, we got told the opposite. "Be generous and giving." In healing anxiety, fairness and healthy self-esteem are preferred.

LOW SELF-ESTEEM GIVING
- Saying yes without consideration for self

- Saying yes after being pressured for the 2nd, 3rd or 4th time
- Trying to do everything yourself
- Saying sorry over and over until you are granted forgiveness
- Apologising for setting a boundary
- Feeling guilty for looking after yourself
- Serving others without boundaries and regretting it

HEALTHY SELF-ESTEEM GIVING AND TAKING

- Considering your needs before saying yes or no
- Delaying your answer to make a conscious decision
- Having goals that are just for you, including nurturing activities
- Following through on your intention to rest
- Saying no while offering another solution: "Thanks, I have plans already. Would next Thursday work instead?"
- Saying yes to fair working conditions and pay from an employer
- Offering fair terms to your employees
- Balancing your needs with other people's requests

HOW MUCH IS ENOUGH?

At the moment of anger, you switch from low self-esteem to extreme high self-esteem, blurting out everything you had kept repressed and hidden for weeks, months or years. In these acute moments of self-importance, you are angry, making up for the times words were kept inside to satisfy other people's happiness.

We need to get real and ask these questions:

- How much can I give that is fair?
- How much can I give and still be peaceful?
- What does my partner need most?
- Are there needs that can be clearly communicated?

However hard it is to say "no" indicates the level of anxiousness. There will be a specific person or group of people you feel as if you are letting down. With a soft heart and open mind, ponder this question for 24 hours. Is it really that big a deal to say no? The purpose of exploring this idea is to not let an anxious story dictate our behaviour.

Is it okay to have 'me time' while missing a friend's dinner party? If you miss a social dinner, the worst that happens is you don't have a meal together. That's it. You had plans to rest and will see them next time. The relationship may not be as fragile as you think but if not attending does cause a problem, then there are bigger issues behind that.

BOUNDARY MANIPULATION

If you feel it is time to prioritise yourself, be aware of those who cross boundaries. They will manipulate and test your resolve. When you say no, they keep trying to get their way. Their methods to convince you could be like a mosquito. You don't notice its penetrative needle, until it's already stung.

- "It won't take long. Come on!" Manipulation
- "Just once more." Manipulation
- "You did it for me last time." Guilt
- "After all I've done for you." Guilt

There are several ways to protect your relationships AND stop people even getting a chance to manipulate. Turning down someone's offer doesn't have to feel like rejection either. Let's explore some elite boundary setting techniques and ways to say no thank you.

Avoid the phrase "I can't" when rejecting somebody's offer. It leaves the door open for them to question "Why?" Because of being asked to explain ourselves, we are on the backfoot. Rather than fielding questions I advise to give an airtight reason upfront.

1) Include the airtight reason. I have plans already to meet my

sister and attend ABC appointment. 2) Give them another option. Would catching up by phone to discuss the plan, work for you on Thursday? 3) Thank you so much for your original offer and thinking of me.

Put planning into your boundary **so it is strong first time**. Having plans to meet somebody or attend an appointment will rarely get questioned, especially when you add the 2nd and 3rd steps. Giving them an alternative date to catch up and thank you, means they get to save face. They weren't rejected. They just got an invitation and gratitude.

> *Appreciating someone for an invite and suggesting an alternative won't even feel like a rejection to them, so you can look after your relationships and avoid having your boundary crossed.*

SPECIFIC BOUNDARIES

Boundaries are a way to set personal rules and ask for care. It's easy enough to think about setting a boundary however making it happen has complexities. What details should be included? How often do I enforce it? What are the ways to make the boundary understood by others? How do I respond when an important boundary is broken?

A boundary related to safety is always top priority. If you find someone disagreeing with a safety-based boundary, consider creating space between you and this person. Having to explain the reasons for yours or someone else's safety, is an overwhelming red flag.

A dangerous person tests boundaries, to find a weak spot. At an early opportunity they use manipulation tactics, projecting guilt and insults. They point out that we are unreasonable or a hypocrite, in an attempt to make us surrender our boundary. In extreme cases seek support to enforce a boundary, like help from family members or the police.

If some of the softer communication about respect is not going well, move onto these firmer boundary setting principles.

STEP 1. SETTING OF THE BOUNDARY.

A detailed boundary is better than a vague one. Include a clear location and time criteria. Take the time to make sure your boundary has necessary details. Communication will best be firm, not casual in this instance. It is worth writing the boundary down too, with the time you told the relevant person. This is gives you a record that cannot be disputed later.

- ~~Stop calling me!~~ Or the following…
- This message is to let you know I won't be accepting phone calls today and tomorrow. After this time, I will make contact to let you know my decision. If you persist in messaging and calling, you will be blocked and I will make a statement to the authorities regarding harassment.
- ~~Stop touching me!~~ Or the following…
- At work a respectful handshake is okay but all other physical contact are off limits. I'm not comfortable with hugs and cheek kisses at my job. Stop from this point forward.

You can give a short window of time for making sure the boundary is understood. When crossed once due to forgetfulness or a mix-up, we remind them straight away. Allow 1 occasion to remind people, after that consequences will be needed to enforce the boundary.

ENFORCEMENT OF THE BOUNDARY STOPS THE SITUATION RECURRING

A boundary not enforced is like a wall of thin air. It supposedly exists but when tested, nothing stops a high self-esteem person continuing their behaviour. Most boundaries will be tested. Sometimes subtly and sometimes dangerously.

When the crossing of a boundary is obvious, repetitive and deliberate, it's a wake-up call that this person feels they can do whatever they want. They do not care about your words. The high self-esteem person crosses boundaries and the low self-esteem person gets walked all over, not wanting to cause a fuss.

"Oh of course I'll rush over there on my day off and take on everybody's responsibility, while getting treated like crap. Let me pander to your needs while mine are ignored. I'd love to help out more, while I'm exhausted. Here's the last of my energy, time and money to make you happy."

STEP 2: ENFORCING THE BOUNDARY

The perpetrator is at fault however we need the skill of enforcing boundaries to protect ourselves. We stop believing that risky people will change their ways. There is no more single important thing than protecting yourself and your family. In doing so, we are on the healing path, building healthy self-esteem.

A boundary that is respected by the other person is a credit to their character. They agreed to your terms and cared enough to follow-through.

HOW DO I ENFORCE A BOUNDARY? ALWAYS WITH CONSEQUENCES.

The purpose of boundary enforcement is to deny the opportunity for it to be crossed again. An example of this would be changing your locks preventing access to an ex-partner that continues to visit unannounced, despite being asked not to.

The power of enforcement is felt by the other person. It does not require words. It requires consequences derived from action. Like a wall blocking someone's path. The wall does not speak but it conveys, "I am a barrier, this behaviour is no longer welcome."

Enforcing a boundary takes much more physical, emotional and mental energy than setting it. Reclaiming one's power will take an increase in energy higher than the person crossing the boundary. You enforce a boundary by denying someone the opportunity to cross it again. A boundary it set and enforced. Your boundary needs weight behind it.

When a boundary is crossed the person needs to know that it was unacceptable behaviour. Actual real-life consequences are the clearest form of communication. The consequences for a boundary crossed can be proportional to the infringement. Lower or higher depending on the situation.

- A family member continues to judge and criticise you on the phone. You hang up. They message to abuse you further by text. How lovely. You block them.
- Gold Coast drivers caught 'hooning' can have their car destroyed by the police. The 'hoons' continued to drive dangerously after many warnings, fines, crashes and even loss of licence. The final enforcement is to crush the car giving no further opportunity for illegal driving.

Enforcing the boundary does not include asking them one more time to please show the deserved respect. "Maybe they'll finally show the care I deserve after the 15th time or the 150th time." They won't. Enforcing the boundary is a leap forward in self-respect. Avoid the trap of continually explaining the boundary to whom clearly ignored it the first time.

If this is your first time enforcing a boundary and I know, for some of you it will be. You could be nervous. This is the low self-esteem talking. You believe other's feelings are more important than yours. The truth is all people are equally important. I'm no more important than you, and you are no more than I.

It comes down to basic human fairness. You can ask yourself inside, "Is this person being fair AND caring?" When someone crosses a boundary, they are showing a willingness to ignore respectful behaviour. I'll only give you straight talk in this book. We do not need to put up with their terrible behaviour.

The upside of enforcing boundaries is you are not anxious and exhausted. Using words, shifted to doing what was needed to protect yourself. Motivation will return to accomplish your goals now. The alternative is to be dumped on and feeling trapped by someone else's intention for your life.

Really, the only reason not to enforce a boundary is an emergency situation. Let's say someone contacts you against your wishes but did so because a family member is in the hospital. Another example could be if an urgent contract has to be submitted and there a legal and financial penalties for not doing this. By all means these exceptions can be allowed.

You could write exceptions in your clearly written boundary. Include who is involved, where the boundary is, how long it will be in place for and exceptions (for emergencies). You can also ask them to confirm they understand what you have said.

Set the detailed boundary. Enforce it firmly.

OBSESSIVE COMPULSIVE DISORDERS

The first part of compulsive disorders are the unwanted, negative thoughts. These include: Shame, overthinking, pessimism, regret, distressing imagery, and beliefs of not being enough. Alongside these thoughts are urges to act against one's own interest.

The second half of OCDs are the rituals. These are actions performed to make the urges cease: Fixation on perfection, creating order & symmetry, hoarding possessions and repetitive actions (checking, tapping, washing, correcting and counting).

An OCD is a type of anxiety that includes rituals. Imagine being deeply worried about finances whilst also suffering with a hoarding ritual. Money problems are made so much worse by compulsively spending, resulting in further anxiety. Emotionally, the person feels momentary accomplishment when purchasing but afterwards burdened. Getting ahead seems impossible.

Once inside a retail store, the mind must have its reward. It's not actually an accomplishment however feels like one because shopping is linked to dopamine release. We know it is responsible to set financial limits but to an OCD sufferer it is not satisfying the urges inside.

HEALING ANXIETY

Everybody says, "Just stop spending, your debt is too much. The credit cards are maxed out." The anxious person tries delaying tactics but finds themselves ready to buy online with a pay later service. More spending and items to accumulate = more success.

Being responsible does not create the desired dopamine reward whereas hoarding temporarily fills the void. A hoarding OCD can even link with identity. "I am my stuff." Or more accurately, "my stuff is what gives me security, worth and purpose. Without it I'm unsure how to function."

The mind is addicted to short-term highs and distractions caused by anxiety. The mind can also be very skilled in avoiding one's problems, with the wrong stuff. It is very important to understand that a compulsive ritual will not heal anxiety. What doesn't work, feels relieving for a few moments but is not a healing action.

OCD is a disorder because the compulsive behaviours do not get rid of anxiety, they reinforce it. It's anxiety with a ritual that is also distressing. If I feel terrible after a certain behaviour or it damages part of my life, that's not in alignment with my healing. An unhealthy behaviour can be recognised by its damaging after-effect.

A common compulsion is feeling guilty about food habits but then overeating for the dopamine reward and stress relief, from that emotion. Sweet food is associated with both guilt and comfort. It's cyclical.

I have never felt terribly guilty for meditating, eating well, going for a run, drinking water and being responsible. What works are balanced behaviours that leave you feeling light, satisfied and healthy afterwards. Obsessive thoughts and anxiety are what compel the person to act in an extreme manner, against their own wellness.

In this chapter I will offer new ways to think about anxiety and OCD. You will discover that rituals can be **part of the healing process**. An enjoyable ritual that you choose is possible rather than a compulsive behaviour that is distressing you. The goal is to reduce the frequency of obsessive thoughts and simultaneously build strength to not act on them.

Important note: Almost all of us have the following behaviours. This does not mean we have OCD. An occasional behaviour that is comforting or quirky, is part of being human. When it becomes a stressful, time-consuming ritual, damaging part of your life, then OCD is more likely and healing required.

> *"All types of OCD include obsessions and compulsions. Obsessions are unwanted and intrusive thoughts, feelings, urges and doubts, while compulsions are repetitive physical or mental actions performed in an attempt to relieve distress and anxiety."*
> **Dr Gary Van Dalfsen**

OCD occurs when intrusive thoughts guide our actions:

- Obsessive thoughts that are moderately difficult to ignore.
- Obsessive thoughts that are very difficult to ignore.
- Obsessive thoughts acted upon frequently or every time.

1. HOARDING COMPULSION

This is a behaviour that many people with OCD have. Hoarding is described as 'collecting and keeping things with little value or usefulness.' An extreme desire to shop/collect, despite it straining their health, relationships, finances and home life, points to a disorder.

While collecting material possessions on its own does not confirm a diagnosis, having another symptom, such as fixation on objects, compulsive shopping or depression, makes OCD more likely. The challenge is to take control of anxious purchasing. Shopping that is measured and enjoyable is fine.

2. REQUIRING ORDER

Those with OCD are compelled to have things ordered a certain way. This behaviour could include arranging stationary evenly apart, lining up books so the heights are level and stacking cans with the barcodes faced away. People with this compulsion experience intense stress when objects are not orderly.

The behaviour could include following the same route to and from work or putting on clothes in a particular way. Basically, you need things to be 'just so' to avoid an anxiety attack or if having one, 'order' is used in an attempt to calm down. When emotions feel like chaos, order makes life temporarily okay.

3. FEAR OF CONTAMINATION

Avoidance of germs is the most common symptom seen in OCD. Those that struggle with fear of germs become distressed to handle items that other people have touched, like doorknobs and bin lids. They may avoid hugging, shaking hands and touching. It is common for OCD sufferers to fear making others sick and not being perfect or moral enough.

Fear of contamination symptoms are often linked with frequent hand washing. We are taught to wash with anti-bacterial soap and hand sanitizer, to avoid getting sick and spreading viruses. Measured cleaning is a normal behaviour, whereas 'fixation' on germs points to a disorder.

4. DOUBLE-CHECKING

Those with obsessive-compulsive disorder struggle with excessive checking. This could result in returning ten or twenty times to make sure the stove switch is off and the house door locked. Checking can be driven by a variety of obsessions, ranging from a high focus on safety or 'needing to be perfect.'

If this behaviour occurs occasionally, it is not reason for concern, but if the ritual interrupts daily life, it may be caused by a deep-rooted issue. Why don't I have confidence in my actions? Does mistrust keep showing up in my life? Is there high stress, so I try to control everything?

5. FOOD OBSESSION

Consider the self-talk used when obsessed with dieting. 'On the bandwagon' represents near perfect choices, regular weight checking but is too restrictive. 'Fallen off the bandwagon' means the pressure is released, eating what one wants and over-indulging on comforting food and drinks. Both restriction and indulgence are opposite extremes. What am I going to have for dinner now? Am I even eating the right food? Why do I keep doing this?

Rather than this uninspiring and obsessive 'bandwagon' phrasing, change self-talk to: I choose food than nurtures my body and mind. My eating plan is based on digestion ease, nutrition and energy. Food is used to satisfy natural hunger. The beauty of the word balance is no one can be addicted to it. Balance is the middle, both in actions and thought process. Emotionally it feels more stable to be balanced.

6. MENTAL GAMES

Those with OCD may have a habit of playing mental games. This symptom is often linked with the counting compulsion. The 'internal rituals,' are not noticeable to those around them however the person may appear distracted. They may count to a specific number because they feel an unusual responsibility to prevent something bad from happening.

"I need to tap the door four times. This means I have protected a loved one or stopped a plane from falling out of the sky." Other examples include counting the steps walking into work or adding the value of letters that make up a word. W = 23 O = 15 R = 18 D = 4. Counting behaviours can be influenced by superstitions. There are good numbers and bad numbers, lucky and unlucky. Avoiding number 13 is an example of this.

7. CONSTANT REASSURANCE

One of the reasons why people with OCD repeat a behaviour is for reassurance. When an individual checks the stove multiple times, it is to be assured that they and others are safe. Sometimes the initial check isn't enough to provide relief, so they go back again. The checking is not based on practicality but reducing anxiety. If checking twice does not appease the mind, then the behaviour is compulsive.

This OCD can include seeking social reassurance, like asking for details about what happened at the party. They want affirmation that no one judged them as weird. The habit of needing reassurance is driven by a fear of rejection and not wanting to appear foolish in the eyes of others.

8. MEMORY HOARDING

Memory hoarding is a mental compulsion to fixate on the details of an event, person, or situation in an attempt to protect themselves from something bad happening. Those who hoard memories believe they will need to recall those thoughts in 100 percent accuracy. Have you ever thought over the details of an argument a dozen times? How about hundreds?

Those going over the details of relationships are fixated on what the other person did/said wrong or what they themselves did/said wrong. Someone with OCD who is engaging in memory hoarding is likely to feel trapped in not moving on from the past. They may not be able to take in the fullness of the present moment.

9. SEXUAL OBSESSIONS

While everyone has had a fantasy, those with OCD will experience sexual obsessions involving forbidden themes to the person: sexual abuse, incest, cheating on a partner, prostitution, self-defecation, rough sex, gay sex, straight sex or unusual sex. However, it's important to note that while the OCD sufferer has these kinds of thoughts, it doesn't mean they will act on them.

The person will find obsession lies somewhere between naughty and disturbing. Thoughts about crossing a moral boundary activate the reward centre of the brain. Men and women experience obsessions at about the same rates. Male or female, religious or not, younger or older will experience sexual fantasies similarly.

10. FIXATING ON LOOKS

It is common for those with obsessive-compulsive disorder to fixate on their appearance in an extreme way. The condition includes fixation and judging part of their body they are unhappy with. Almost everyone has some sort of physical insecurity, but it could become a sign of OCD if this insecurity leads to hours a day of checking the mirror and ruminating on it.

Fixation could also relate to their clothing, partner, family, pet, car and house appearance. The constant act of making something better takes away from appreciating what is wonderful in the present moment. Even when approaching perfection, fear of losing physical beauty looms in the background. Every 'body' has wonderful physical attributes that can be appreciated.

HALEY'S STORY

Haley was a 20-year-old university student. She lived in their family home with her parents, sister and had a boyfriend visit occasionally. Haley feared uncleanliness and germs. She described to me panic and disgust when the following occur.

- Family preparing and eating meat
- People licking their fingers
- Anyone entering her bedroom
- Boyfriend in her bedroom (not showered or dirty)
- Anyone handling rubbish
- Unhygienic behaviour
- General sweatiness and dirtiness

She struggled to tolerate loved ones around the dinner table. Her family ate "disgusting meals, touched their faces and kitchen surfaces." After dinner they opened the bin with their hands to discard scraps. She checked intensely that everyone washed properly. Things were not right, according to her perspective.

Haley criticised loved one's hygiene but judged her obsessiveness more. Haley wished for enjoyment with family and to just be relaxed. Sometimes she managed to stay calm. Other times anxiety was too much and retreated to her clean bedroom sanctuary.

She said with a tone of tiredness: "There is no need for me to worry so much about how clean things are, it is draining my joy. The fear of germs is always there. Some days it affects me less and other times it is overwhelming."

After some discussion I introduced Haley to the Law of Opposites – Duality – Balance. That which exists also does not. That which is expressed is repressed. Any behaviour performed to a high degree will have an equal expression, at the opposite end of the behaviour spectrum. We will go deep on this topic in the Balance Section of this book.

If someone is very clean, where are they messy? If someone says they are always punctual, when are they late? If someone is a hoarder, what do they easily let go off; physically, mentally, emotionally or materially? Or if someone is not sexual, where do they express it; in fantasy, romance novels, writing, self-pleasure, kinks and taboos?

Back to Haley: The problem will be perceived as all-encompassing by the client however after an examination of reality, it won't be. I wanted to show Haley how the law of opposites applied to her case. I was curious to check how often the anxiety about germs was 'not there.' I encouraged her to remember instances where she got messy or dirty and was 'okay with it.'

Me: "No behaviour occurs around the clock, 24 hours a day. The mind is not like that. It can switch off and change focus. I wonder if there are already times you remember being free of worry Hayley. Where and with whom, don't you obsess about cleanliness?"

Haley replied quite quickly: "Oh, at the gym, definitely. I use the equipment and get sweaty and it doesn't even bother me."

I enquired: "How many times do you use the gym each week?"

Haley: "2-3 times, it's at the university. I touch the equipment and just shower afterwards."

Me: "Great, no anxiety in that situation. Where else and with whom?"

Haley: "Jumping in the pool and playing games with my family."

Me: "Is that fun and enjoyable and there's times where you are actually relaxed."

Haley: "Oh, definitely."

Me: "Any other times?"

Haley thinking for a few moments now: "Having sex. I mean, I know my boyfriend is not 100% clean after a shower, no one is. So, I allow germs when he comes over sometimes."

She went on… "Oh, and this is a huge one. When I have burgers or pizza I eat with my fingers, and for some reason its fine."

Me: "Why is that? What are the circumstances?"

Haley: "Usually I'm with friends. There is a group of us and we go out somewhere. They eat burgers with their hands too and it doesn't bother me at all."

Her mind opened up a bit. Anxiety about germs was not happening all the time. It occurred sometimes. Around family it was higher but with people her own age, when exercising and having fun, anxiety about germs was significantly less.

Haley was becoming aware of freedom in several situations. We had just reduced anxiety from being all-encompassing, to something that happens on occasion. Without even having to try, her mind is entirely capable of turning OCD down or off and this gives hope that freedom can flow into her life.

Me: "Can you see that being dirty sometimes, mucking around and having fun are the best bits in life?"

She searched her mind for anything that was clean and fun for a long while. It seemed the majority of good times occur when there could be

HEALING ANXIETY

germs! Hanging out with friends, gym, eating burgers and pizza, sex and socialising. I concluded from her ongoing pondering that she couldn't think of a single time when fun and germs didn't go together.

Me: "Do the best bits in life happen when there could be germs?" I didn't ask any more questions and just let the idea play out for her.

After searching every corner of her mind, Haley realised out loud, "I don't have a fear of germs and I worry not living to the fullest, because of anxiety."

Me: "When others are unclean, I wonder if they are relaxed and having fun. Would you rather be perfectly clean or have peace?"

Another door opened in her mind. She enjoyed herself most when a little bit sweaty or dirty. Yes, Haley feared germs but there was a strong void of missing out, because of that fear. The battle was not with germs. The battle was anxiety itself. Trying to achieve perfect cleanliness is not a reasonable goal that's why it's obsessive; trying to control the uncontrollable; and achieve the unachievable.

The pressure is released around people her age, probably to get acceptance from the group. She couldn't even think of fun that didn't include possible germs. Space for healing inside her mind was expanding. There is freedom to express herself and room for others too. Good hygiene practice is responsible but it does not need to be a full-time job.

Haley: "Ensuring the cleanliness of others is not my role in the world. When sharing a meal my intention is fun and connection. This is my ritual now. I can focus on my enjoyment in the present. I acknowledge that little feelings of anxiety are okay. I'm not going to fight it anymore."

Haley created a mental ritual of focusing on what she wants. Cleanliness is only a problem when the dose is too high and it is obsessive. An extreme level of cleaning (due to germaphobia) is exhausting but a moderate level of personal hygiene takes care of safety. It is still wise to take care of your responsibilities within reason.

Affirmation: "I am clean enough. Others are clean enough. I am okay."

Affirmation: "I clean responsibly. I clean in proportion. I clean when relaxed."

Affirmation: "A ritual I choose and love = freedom."

OLD RITUAL

The thought, "What if the front door is not locked?" is okay. You check it is secure and leave for the day. However, if you get in your car and the thought, "What if the front door is unlocked?" becomes obsessive and is re-checked a specific number of times, that is OCD.

We don't overcome anxious patterns by judging them as bad however taking on new ways of behaving that support body and mind wellness. Rituals can be uplifting when they are useful and chosen by you. The approach we continue to focus on is **healing anxiety** and **not fighting anxiety**.

We will expand your OCD responses to include a healthy ritual. Breathing in a steady rhythm during meditation is an example of a positive ritual. Turning an anxious morning routine into something healthy, fun and organised, is another possibility.

Considerations for choosing a ritual:

- Check it is healthy for the body and mind
- Check the new ritual is fun or uplifting
- Make it shorter or longer in time as you desire
- Include an affirmation
- Breathe and notice nothing bad happens

Let's examine the ritual of re-checking when leaving for work in the morning. A person walks to the car, then back up the stairs and checks the front door is locked 15 times. It's such a waste of energy and being late for work makes anxiety worse.

NEW RITUAL

When leaving the house, I will change anxiety about checking the front door into a fun song.

"1 2 3 4 close the door. 5 6 7 8 locked and now I am feeling great.

9 10 11 12 haha how funny it is to rhyme 12 with 12. Who cares? 13 14 15 happy as I ever have been. Checked the door just one time, that's the end of my funny rhyme." Be present to the sound of the lock clicking. Smile and walk joyfully towards the car.

Walking or skipping joyfully can be added to any ritual, using the body to create a positive mood. Because checking the door had previously been done 15 times, we included counting to fifteen in this new ritual. If you like nursery rhymes use that and have fun with it. "Twinkle twinkle little lock, how I love you in the right spot, just in line, feeling fine, glad I'll make it to work on time."

Notice that we are not fighting anxiety here. We are working with our human nature to act in patterns. The re-checking was so obsessive previously. We switch the energy around using humour, rhyming and moving your body in a fun way. Physical and emotional experiences create neural connections faster. A behaviour you find rewarding makes change happen even quicker and more likely for the long term.

Humour, rhyming and skipping to the car are things you have never done in combination and not in the context of going to work at 8:00am. Doing new, interesting behaviours can 'positively jolt' the mind into thinking differently and therefore feeling differently. Make the ritual your own, with expression you enjoy.

There are no limits to the creativity that can be used in your new ritual. Use all the senses. You could add a cup of tea or an essential oil like lavender, in the morning. A favourite song could be played with your healthy ritual or an affirmation like, "In the present moment I am lovable. I love my unique qualities."

There is no downside doing this. The worst that happens by incorporating healthy and light behaviours is your day gets better. It is an opportunity to change your mood and rewire the brain for behaviour change. And that's just how you do it. You literally do different things that make you feel good.

Create a new ritual where you stop beating yourself up in a negative spiral. Add actions you find soft, light and fun! We are intervening on an OCD you want to be free of. Real relief is possible by taking back control of your **thoughts** and **rituals**.

Identify a situation or time of day that triggers an unwanted compulsive behaviour. Perform a new healing ritual when the old OCD pattern used to occur. A quality ritual can be implemented at a specific location and time with great effect. For example, the living room at 8:00am. The new pattern can leave you feeling empowered, safe and healthy.

Rituals you can start today:

- Pleasant morning ritual
- Gratitude ritual
- Breathing/meditation ritual
- Self-care or spiritual activities
- Fun activities
- Evening ritual after work

OPPORTUNITY RITUALS

Rituals might seem like an additional burden on the mind. They aren't. It is empowering that you choose, rather than be controlled by obsessive rituals. We want to fill the gap of the old repetitive actions with something that matches your goals and personality. Use a ritual that you believe in and adds value to your life.

Attention to details could become a career in, accounting, landscape gardening, composing music, cleaning, art or proofreading. Self-punishment could become self-exploration of the spiritual, your mind, body, needs or desires. Gambling compulsion could become studying the housing, stock and financial markets to become wealthier.

For Haley, freedom from and 'obsessive cleanliness' involved leaning into the idea that dirtiness and possibility of germs are okay. Friends, family and a boyfriend are a natural and fun part of life. The opportunity she found was to focus on enjoying herself at these times and no longer fighting anxiety.

HEALING YOUR ANXIETY

With any anxiety we are in one of these stages on the healing spectrum.

- Stopped working on healing
- Avoiding triggers and issues
- Resisting anxiety
- Healed or healing the anxiety

STOPPED WORKING ON HEALING

After years of frustration and disappointment we succumb to the situation we find ourselves. At one end of the healing spectrum, the bottom, thoughts and feelings are disregarded. I power on with unhealthy behaviours. I am angry at myself and others. Behind that anger is fear. Something will always go wrong. I'm not enough. Everyone will see who I am and reject me.

There is temporary relief in giving up on healing. I don't have to try so hard any-more. Time will solve my problems (I hope), yet no plan exists to take back control. Self-care and mindfulness are minimal. Sleep and energy are suffering and the nervous system frazzled. Mostly I expect to fail. Unfortunately, the anxiety remains over the long-term. The belief is I can't do anything about it.

AVOIDING TRIGGERS AND ISSUES

The avoidance strategy is limited and passive. I believe if I just keep my head down and avoid anxious situations, it will be okay. I don't like confrontations with family or at work. When I avoid issues too long, food binging, drinking alcohol and medications are resorted to. Healthy avoidance looks like, taking a break, nature, music, reading and space to oneself.

There is a fine line between empowering and disempowering avoidance. In example 1, if I avoid discussing important issues with my partner, I'm not dealing with my marriage and nothing changes. Avoiding communication is an opportunity missed. In example 2, if I say no to a social gathering, 'getting rotten drunk and then ashamed,' that is healthy and empowering. If avoidance is responsible and beneficial, it is a healing action.

RESISTING ANXIETY

Those who are resisting anxiety have decided, enough of this. The fight back for healing has begun. This can include exercise and setting goals for myself. I start speaking up for my rights at work and home. The resisting phase is necessary and useful short term. I start to challenge the source of anxious thoughts. I am not my anxious thoughts! I am going to heal!

Resisting anxiety can become an unwanted pattern. For example, fighting for one's rights, makes change happen. I just don't want to get stuck in a war, fighting myself and others endlessly. At it's best, resisting anxiety is getting fired up, to live a better life. We say no to self-limiting beliefs and other people's drama. To get out of the resisting phase, switch over to the healing phase.

HEALING ANXIETY

At this end of the spectrum we focus on fundamentals that heal anxiety; safety, truth, confidence and self-acceptance. I take responsibility for my role in the healing process. I set goals that are in alignment with my highest values. I take action promptly in hours or days as opposed to procrastination for months or years. I use the guidance of physical and mental health professionals. I bring my mind attention to the present moment.

In the present moment I accept myself, others and even anxiety as they are (resisting who I am, others and anxiety is still in the fighting phase). I work towards a healthy self-esteem. I don't place others above or below me. I focus on leadership, rather than blame and worry. I make choices based on what serves myself and others fairly. I utilise mindfulness, exercise and healing when overwhelmed.

WHAT IS WRONG WITH FIGHTING ANXIETY?

"It's bad. I can't stand anxiety!" To put it plainly we don't feel good when we are fighting. The act of resisting creates tension. This is true in physics and psychology. To stop fighting, we need to change the paradigm we think and act from. Judging myself and others made up 20 years of my life and it didn't help me progress.

Healing on the other hand is both improving our situation and we feel good, on the journey. The path taken and result are both important. If your method of anxiety reduction is dangerous or stressful, strongly consider another option. Healing actions generally make you feel good, while you are doing it.

A lady I met recently took a quality healing action instead of fighting. Work drama was making her anxious. She decided not to resist it anymore. She said to her gossiping co-workers, "I'm going back to work now." She turned around, walked away and didn't give them a second thought. Rather than fighting and trying to change them, she focused on her mission, which is serving people.

You might be ashamed it took so long to do what is needed. That's resisting the past. A prompt action in the healing direction is a breakthrough you can be proud of. In the present moment you can acknowledge a great achievement on your part. Every single time you have a doubt and take a healing action, you are healing.

Short mindfulness process: "Hi anxiety thanks for the brief visit. Do you have anything useful for me today? Pause. Gladly provide me with some useful thoughts or bugger off. Pause. Come back if you have something helpful to say, I'm getting back to what I love now."

Someone who is healed or healing, may still experience anxiety, from time to time. Anxious thoughts are allowed to flow in and out of the mind. They don't engage the thoughts with battle. They accept that anxiety exists and use healing principles. They add more safety, confidence (knowledge, action, support, truth, alignment) and self-acceptance.

By taking action you initiate a healing possibility.

Each time you achieve gains, be proud of yourself. If an anxious episode used to be 5 hours and now lasts 10 minutes, that is huge progress. If anxiety used to be 9/10 intensity and now it is a 1/10 or a 4/10, celebrate these wins. Over time, anxiety and panic attacks will become shorter and milder. Healing may happen right away or be a progression.

PRESENT MOMENT ENJOYMENT

We want anxiety under control and have other life goals too. The purpose of healing is to have freedom to do more of what we want. The focus can **shift away** from anxiety, to what you value, in the present moment. If you are currently using positive thinking strategies or would like to start, here is a way to create your outcome quicker.

- If excited about the prospect of becoming healthier, say "My body is healing in this moment. I love my body." Allow an hour a day for looking after yourself. Drink a glass of water and create a meal plan, in the present moment. Seek out a health practitioner

for support. You are in alignment when you are both saying it and doing it.
- If looking forward to a relaxing holiday, spend a little time resting now. Have a lunch break outside, in the sunshine. Block out dates in your calendar and start putting money aside for your trip. Don't wait until your official holiday before finding a break time. Enjoy relaxation in the present moment too.
- If excited about a dream job, say, "I am a great candidate. I have a lot to offer now." Call and email the company to learn about what is required for the role. Learn about the company's core values. This knowledge helps you be confident the job is aligned with your personality and goals. Complete any courses that are needed.

A present moment activity makes your visualisation a reality. Getting it done, or making progress towards the goal makes you powerful. When something is your top priority, don't let anxiety interfere with it. Is this the difference between anxious procrastinators and successful creators? They take action towards what they want, in the present.

Anxiety has us thinking about all the what ifs and procrastinating. **Waiting** to do what I love doesn't feel good and at some level fear is behind it. What am I waiting for? Could I get the ball get rolling with one little push? Is there a step I can complete **today**? Who or what deserves my love and attention?

> *"Every value pertaining to life requires action to maintain it. If we do not continue to breathe, the breathing we did yesterday will not keep us alive today. The same principle applies to self-esteem and the practices that support it."*
> **Nathaniel Branden**

A guideline to follow. Today is best, tomorrow is good. Longer than 48 hours and the energy changes. Creative energy works best alongside a physical expression. Imagine if someone thought their whole life about changing careers or doing what they really love and never got around to it. Depression and illness are two such outcomes of repressed energy.

If I have been worrying about ABC issue regularly, then there is a reason for that. My thoughts become conscious for the purpose of healing them. Action is what turns worry, into healing. When I call my thoughts bad and avoid them, the process is incomplete. A present moment opportunity was missed to create the life I intended.

MONKEY MIND

In the book 'Leaving The OCD Circus,' Kirsten described her anxiety as a Drill Sergeant, barking orders that must be completed to perfection. The threats this overlord character would make, were pictures of her family meeting violent deaths. "Something bad will happen because of you." An inability to stop the images, meant OCD was ruling her life.

Kirsten's anxiety and OCD was:

- Time consuming
- Risked her safety
- Physically exhausting
- Not healing anxiety
- Hidden from those around her

Kirsten was in the category of not working on healing. The main strategy was to complete obsessive rituals, to stop Drill Sergeant (who only exists in her imagination)! It was all too much and for two decades there was not a single person who knew what she was going through, let alone a professional that was supporting her.

The only thing that made the gruesome images cease, was to perform time-consuming rituals. Unplugging and re-plugging household appliances several times was an example. Tapping her finger on a surface with perfect rhythm and perfect pressure 40 times, was another. She would also unscrew and screw back in all the lightbulbs.

One day at home there was a very high lightbulb she had never noticed. Drill Sergeant immediately demanded she perform the unscrewing/screwing ritual perfectly for this lightbulb. The fitting was high, so getting to it required climbing on top of household items. Kirsten slipped and fell onto a glass terrarium. She was thankfully uninjured but one of the glass shards sliced her hamster's head clean off.

Every time the tasks were performed to avoid violent images, it unfortunately gave her power away. The rituals took several hours per day and did not increase her safety, self-acceptance and confidence. Ironically doing the rituals to avoid images of death, resulted in the demise of a beloved pet.

> *OCD cost her time, wellbeing and the life of a hamster.*

Kirsten, with assistance from a therapist began to slowly challenge the anxious thoughts. Over time routines were changed to take back control. She would go shopping, feel the anxiety but afterwards note "nothing bad happened." Later, anxiety was represented in her mind as a wild monkey rather than a threatening Drill Sergeant. My thoughts are wild, is better than disturbing commands and threats.

COMBINATION RITUALS

A combination ritual is a habit with several benefits, provided by the one action. When assisting clients to change a pattern of anxiety, we discuss lifestyle and healing possibilities. Some rituals are very beneficial and can solve a few problems at once.

If your ritual solves several problems at once and is healthy, that is very special indeed. My morning routine of drinking hot water with lemon hydrates me, wakes me up and is good for kidney health. I appreciate the multiple benefits it provides.

A GENTLEMAN IN SYDNEY

His mood was low, missed connection with people and desired weight loss. The combination ritual he discovered was to walk along the river. The sunshine and water enhanced mood and he always chatted to people in the area. The ritual boosted him emotionally, provided useful weight loss and social connection.

A LADY IN BRISBANE

She was stressed, a single mother of 3 kids and the house was messy. The combination ritual used was very creative. Every Sunday, for over a year, she took an hour-long bath. She enjoyed quiet and relaxation. What about the kids? Her 12, 10 and 8 year old children cleaned the whole house. While she had self-nurture time, the kids worked as a team and got the job done.

A LADY IN BRISBANE

She was anxious in the late afternoon, wanted weight loss and her 2 kids (on the autism spectrum) were often fighting. I asked if they do activities together as a family? She said they all used to go for a 4:30pm bike ride but got out of the habit. "Now that I think about it, the kids were way calmer, I enjoyed it and was much slimmer at the time. It really worked well for all of us. I think we'll start again today."

ALTERNATE MEANING TECHNIQUE

The truth can be factual, though several different perspectives can be true. The sky is blue but appears grey when cloudy. At sunrise and sunset the sky can be pink, orange, yellow, red or golden. At night time it is much darker. There is no one correct statement about what colour the sky is. It depends on timing and point of view.

The mind interprets limited information and then delivers us meaning, to understand what is going on in life. The problem with this, is the mind can be **stuck on one perspective** and miss out on other possible explanations. What colour is the sky? Let me consider the whole picture before I give a very limited answer, based on my biases.

The Alternative Meaning Technique finds new ways of interpreting a situation, to give you greater perspective. Some anxiety can be resolved by opening the mind to another idea never previously considered. It is worth considering a wider range of viewpoints, than a narrow focus. Are there different ways of seeing difficult circumstances? What is on the other side of my stubborn mindset?

Both of the following scenarios have happened to me.

SCENARIO 1. REJECTED BY MY FRIEND
Old, unhelpful beliefs:

- Something is wrong with me
- I am unlovable
- This friendship might not continue

New, possible beliefs:

- They need space (for whatever reason)
- They are overwhelmed by something
- They missed my message
- They are prioritising their time
- Our energies aren't aligned at present
- I am a lovable person regardless of no reply
- Time alone can be a blessing
- I enjoy alone time. I'm going for a bushwalk
- I support my friend's decision for space
- I have other people I can visit
- It doesn't mean anything at all that my friend hasn't replied. The meaning is unknown

SCENARIO 2. WRITING MY NEXT BOOK IS TAKING A LONG TIME

Old, unhelpful beliefs:

- I am not a very good writer
- The book might not get finished
- I'm not good enough at this

New, possible beliefs:

- I had temporary writer's block
- After a break, writing gets easier again
- My book will be helpful to millions of people
- Doubt is temporary, my vision is inevitable
- I love writing
- Quality is better than rushing things
- I have been successful writing before, so I will be again
- There are people who will support me
- I am so excited to finish this book
- It doesn't mean anything that the project isn't finished yet

This is the Alternative Meaning Technique in action. You write down the limiting beliefs and then 10-15 plausible, useful alternatives. Your situation always has blessings. It is temporary. Love and acceptance are also possible. The healing-based beliefs are helpful, including true and possibly true perspectives.

NOTE ON IT DOESN'T MEAN ANYTHING:

In both examples, I consider that the situation doesn't mean anything. I immediately relax with this mindset. There is nothing to fix, only a chance to let go of needing any interpretation at all. The situation IS what it IS, which is not fully known. Because the whole situation is not known then there is room for uplifting and healing thoughts.

NOTE ON THE LOVING PERSPECTIVE:

A loving approach is another personal favourite. By loving my friend from a far, I don't have to fix anything. I can wish them well in my heart, whatever their unknown circumstances and let it go. Self-love regarding my book project, means I stop dwelling on the negative and get back in my creative energy. Writing is enjoyable again without the weight of time pressure and self-judgement.

THE WATERFALL

Picture that you are on board a solid wooden raft with a paddle. There is a very gentle current, almost still, at the start of the river. In this position, manoeuvring back ashore is easy. You can control the vessel due to the relative stillness of the water. Downstream, the water flow increases and getting back to safety takes more effort.

The current changes from calm, to rapids and eventually the crest of a waterfall, representing catastrophe (a full-blown anxious episode). In adventure films, the hero doesn't realise there is danger ahead, until it is too late. They become aware suddenly of intensifying water flow and must escape before capsizing. With all their might they grab hold of a rock or grasp an overhanging branch.

There might be early signs you are nearing troubled waters. You become agitated or are in a situation that previous triggered an anxious episode. Your work week might have been overwhelming and have felt emotional pressure building. (not sleeping, loss of appetite, swirling stomach, self-judgement, replaying a negative story in your mind). This is the time for healthy rituals.

Your best wins with healing anxiety will come by stopping an attack from even happening. When the emotional flow is building, guide yourself smoothly back to shore. The sooner you notice symptoms and leave the river, the less resistance is faced downstream.

You don't have to wait until things get out of control before acting. When sensing turbulent emotions, you have become self-aware and can use your tools to get back to the safety of shore. The shore represents mindfulness and your healing rituals. You aren't travelling deeper into anxiety, while you are **healing** on dry land.

Any time you stop an anxious episode from crashing your day is a huge victory and can be celebrated!

When stress is 5/10 - 6/10 I use a healing ritual, until things settle. If stress is higher than that, I make healing a priority, using the rituals at least twice per day. I'll put it in my diary as an appointment. Self-care time 10am-11am. I'll see a professional or use one of the mindfulness techniques outlined, throughout this book.

During acute anxiety the healing rituals you choose, will be your go-to for recovery. There might be one that is just perfect for you or like me a variety of methods are beneficial. During periods of mild or no anxiety the rituals can still be used, for maintaining your physical and mental health. An empowered way of thinking and healthy lifestyle will help keep you afloat.

When should I start being mindful? The present moment is a good time for healing to begin.

MINDFULNESS

Pause in this moment. Unclench the jaw and let your teeth separate. Slowly soften the forehead. Allow your shoulders to release. Breathe deep. Exhale with an audible sigh, "aaah."

Mindfulness is being aware of your needs, breathing and self-talk. Mindfulness for mental health includes being conscious of emotions and strategies to think and feel better.

The limbic system and amygdala are regions of the brain associated with anxiety. They are reactive and send stress hormones into our bloodstream. The amygdala, also referred to as primitive brain, which overrides rational thought.

In an anxious episode the quality of self-talk and breathing are poor. We get hijacked by a kamikaze pilot, trying to crash our day with destructive thoughts. This could be a pattern of judgement, negativity, addiction or ruminating about a story.

The brain regions associated with higher thinking are the cerebrum and prefrontal cortex. Mindfulness will gently shift your physiology away from reaction, back to the reasoning mind. Consciously directing your self-talk and breathing gives you control of 2 key aspects of your state. With practice you can focus your mind on higher functions (like gratefulness and confidence building).

- A cerebrum is active when I am understanding another's point of view different to mine. When I accept both my positive and negative qualities, this too is a cerebrum type response. Thinking is open and non-reactive to the situation.
- The amygdala is associated with fight and flight mode. If I am resisting or avoiding a situation, that is an amygdala response. I have stopped asking quality questions. I am overwhelmed and pessimistic.

How can I take back control from an amygdala hijacker? How do I activate reasonable thinking? Consider the waterfall analogy from the last chapter. When you first notice anxiety, focus on healing, sooner rather than later. Knowing your emotional triggers and settling anxiety quickly, is the healing process at its best.

ASKING THE RIGHT QUESTIONS

Let's start off exploring these mindfulness lessons, by removing what does not work. We have all done it. Maybe even today. It's asking, 'dead end questions.'

I am labelling these 'dead end questions' because they lead to little or no useful conclusion. These internal queries are stressful and related to the primitive mind. Dead end questions surface when feeling powerless.

~~Why am I so ANXIOUS all the time?~~ Delete this question.
~~Why can't I fix this?~~ Delete this question.
~~How did I end up in this mess?~~ Delete this question.
~~Why is this happening to me?~~ Delete this question.
~~What is wrong with me?~~ Delete this question.

The mind answers these types of questions with more stories about why you have anxiety and are not enough. The questions are typically not useful and pre-suppose that something is wrong with you. That is not healing. We want to be free from anxiety and beating ourselves up with dead end self-talk.

Be rid of them for good and shift to higher enquiries. As best you can, be self-aware, asking questions that bring back the reasoning mind. Let's focus now on a different type of internal query that empowers and creates a healing possibility.

EMPOWERING QUESTIONS

The following series of questions are designed to unlock safety, awareness, gratitude, empowerment, love and truth. They will turn you around from the waterfall back to the shore. For the next 7 days start asking and answering these questions for yourself.

Here are the answers I found when navigating relationship stress:

Am I and other people safe? Yes, everyone is safe. Acknowledging that safety is most important lets the mind know you are okay. If protection is needed in a situation, that is always the first step to take. If not safe, make it a priority. Impending risk involving yourself, family, finances, work, health, home and school is top priority. Seek support.

What do I want resolved? I want to be heard. I want to be on the same page with our goals. I want to love and be loved. This question can provide a clear objective to focus on. The answers hinted to a path I can take: **Listen, discuss goals** and **be loving**. My wants are also actions that's embodied.

What am I grateful for? I am grateful I learnt about my partner. I got to express my needs. I appreciate the effort we put in. I am grateful we are communicating openly. Find the blessings of the problem you are working on. Keep answering this question until you feel grateful in your heart.

What would love do now? If I were at my most loving, how would I treat myself and others? Be in heart space in this moment. To experience love, I give it first. I connect with love flowing towards me and to her. I give in the way she wants to receive. When being the provider, give fully in the present moment. Love comes first.

What is true? There was a disagreement. It wasn't that bad. We care about each other. I played my part and took responsibility for that. This question is designed to strip away the story of anxiety. There is a difference between emotional exaggerations and what is true. Practice self-talk with what is 'actually happening?' Not over-playing or down-playing the meaning.

This process may take as little as 5 minutes to complete or you could spend longer in deep reflection. Keep going with the questions until you are clear-minded and soft-hearted.

Prior to answering these questions, I was anxious and reactive. I wanted to be heard. Mindfulness allowed me to listen first and afterwards express my needs calmly. I was ready to have an open conversation. My energy shifted to love and care. I was completely focused on making the situation better.

Mindfulness questions brought about a state of clarity and love.

There is no limit to empowering self-talk. If you are seeing a psychologist, counsellor or hypnotherapist weekly, these questions are great to practise between sessions. To question means to seek, investigate and examine. The purpose of these examinations are to find healing solutions. Here are 8 categories, with a series of higher-minded questions:

SAFETY AND NEEDS
Is the situation safe?
    What are my top needs at present?
    Am I hungry or tired?
    What is anxiety trying to protect me from?

PROBLEM SOLVING
How can I resolve this situation?
    What is the main cause of this problem?
    What can I do, in the present moment?

Do I need more information or support?

ALIGNMENT
Is this job, person or activity in alignment with me?
　What makes me feel lively and fulfilled?
　What is my gut instinct saying?
　When would I genuinely like to leave this social event?

SELF-CARE
Does this food make me feel light and energised afterwards?
　Do my senses need a break from overwhelm?
　How does my body prefer to be nurtured?
　How much rest time do I need this week?

RELATIONSHIPS
Do I need more knowledge to understand this person?
　What do I want to express/get off my chest?
　Are there clear relationship agreements?
　What makes me feel safe in relationships?

PERSPECTIVE
Can I focus on being excellent instead of perfect?
　What mistakes are okay?
　What am I most grateful for today?
　Are my thoughts true (based in reality)?

LOVE
What do I love about me?
　What is important to my heart today?
　Who are all the people whom have ever loved me?
　Which people love to help me?

PRESENCE
Is my mind focus far in the future?
   Is my mind focus too much in the past?
   How is the quality of my breathing?
   Can I be present, doing one thing at a time?

Quality questions → useful answers → better perspective or solution → feeling of accomplishment and relief.

SELF-TALK AND SLEEP
Susan visited my clinic with difficulty falling asleep. She tried to rest in the evenings but found herself getting more agitated, as time wore on. The problem had been occurring for more than a year. I asked how aware she is of her state just before sleep. Is she able to relax physically? How is the quality of self-talk?

Susan revealed, "I am harsh with myself when I can't shut off my mind. I say, what's wrong with you Susan? Just rest!"

'What is wrong with you Susan?' is a dead-end question.

She was both yelling and judging herself, one part of each. I listened to the details and picked up on something out of place. There was a change in her accent compared to how she spoke before. It was slight but caught my attention. I asked the next question based on this, hopefully heading in the right direction.

I inquired, "Something caught my attention. The way you criticise yourself, it sounds like someone else is speaking. Does that mean anything to you? Whose voice is in your head when you try to sleep? Could it have been a parent, former partner or maybe an authority figure? I wonder where this habit of being critical originated."

She thought for a moment and remembered 12 months ago a male doctor was angry with her difficulty in sleeping. "Just relax will you, it's not that hard!" Before this moment, Susan had not made a connection between the doctor and her anxiety. Never had she decided to judge herself this way but when unable to sleep, this was the harsh judgement on replay.

Criticism started with the doctor and was adopted by the mind as a mental habit.

Once mindful of this, she could choose differently. Insomnia, plus self-judgement, was not a ritual she needed to partake of any longer. We chatted about how forceful language from the doctor was on replay, activating the 'sympathetic nervous system' and 'amygdala.'

Ideally self-talk would be relaxing, encouraging the parasympathetic nervous system. Thoughts are slower, softer, accepting and praising of self, particularly in regard to sleep.

I asked Susan to make a list of words that represented lovely sleep. I suggested she use these words twice. The first time shortly before getting into bed and again when lying down, whilst drifting off. Her new sleep ritual utilised the following for the next 7 nights.

- Her self-talk included "peaceful," "drowsy," "deep sleep" and "calm."
- The tone she used was soothing. "I'll drift off in my own time and thaaat's okaaay."
- She complimented herself – "I am doing great."
- The volume of her self-talk was *softer*, like a whisper.
- She completed a few deliberate yawns to prompt the body into drowsiness.

Our physiology is encouraged to relax by affirmations and *how we say them*. The words used, volume and tone are all important.

- Avoid judgemental language
- Adjust the volume of self-talk

- Change the accent from male to female or vice-versa
- Replace the old story with your desired outcome
- Use words aligned with your goal

GLENDA'S HEALTH ANXIETY

Glenda was in her mid-sixties and came to see me about quitting smoking. She reported, "Very high anxiety on a daily basis" yet was determined to put the cigarette habit behind her. Glenda had smoked approximately 30 per day, for 40 years. That's 438,000 cigarettes.

Although smoking was used as a coping mechanism for anxiety, she felt terribly anxious about cigarettes. She had been diagnosed with the early stages of emphysema and was sick of the endless cycle of seeking relief all the while feeling tense.

How can mindfulness assist with quitting smoking? Start by being aware of how your body feels on a regular basis. Notice how the habit has increased anxiety and not healed it. Notice the impact of smoking on state of mind and what it restricts you from. For example, experiencing beautiful health, wealth and family time. Lung illness is a very strong message from the body, that will worsen if ignored.

The addiction cycle can be observed with compulsive behaviours that provide no desired result. Think about the gambler who craves winning yet loses consistently, the comfort food eater that is very uncomfortable with weight gain and Glenda who is wanting relief yet anxious every single day about her lung illness.

Over time, addiction always causes loss. Addictions are hard to control because the mind deludes itself, believing it is the solution to their anxiety. When the brain has associated positive feelings to a damaging habit, drug or medication, it will be craved again and again despite being unsatisfying at a deeper level.

I need cigarettes to relax. How relaxed are you most days? Umm... stressed to the max!

Belief that she would be okay without cigarettes, needed to be stronger than her delusion of addiction being the answer. If cigarettes helped with anxiety, then someone who has smoked 438,000 cigarettes, should be so incredibly calm, relaxed and peaceful but that's nowhere close to reality.

In Glenda's case, this 40 year habit was a distraction from anxiety. A mere 5 minutes of escaping her thoughts. The habit never boosted her safety, confidence or self-acceptance. It had not hydrated or delivered nutrients to her body. It never made her happy, except for brief moments by herself, tuning out from life.

Nicotine replacement products (which are 96% ineffective) and Champix medication (which at time of writing had been banned for dangerous side-effects like hallucination) do nothing to promote healing. Rather than medication, I offered solutions to care for her mind and body that are safe and reliable.

She deserved much better. We all do. I advised seven healthy habits for daily practice. Her body was in near constant anxiety (despite smoking for relaxation). Truly supporting the body would transform her experience.

1. Breathing technique
2. 2.5 litres of water
3. Eating breakfast and regular meals
4. Walking
5. Learning to rest and be still
6. Resilient self-talk
7. Doing what she loves

For the first time in decades Glenda gave her body nurturing. Not chemicals. It makes sense to use these seven strategies because they are compatible with the human body and there is little to no downsides.

With these techniques we are aiming for long-term and realistic well-being. The body heals through 1) breathing to activate the parasympathetic nervous system, 2) hydration, 3) nutrition, 4) exercise, 5) recovery, 6) positive & resilient self-talk and 7) doing what we love every day.

Once you accept a mission of healing, all your decisions flow from this intention. You choose what helps, not harms the body and mind. For some this is the first time in their lives they have committed to nurturing themselves.

Giving up a destructive habit that you have had for 40 years is a big life shift. Emotions of guilt, fear and anger are possible. How could I have done this to myself for so long? These emotions in reality are not bad, just signals that something is very out of balance.

Another downside of the smoking habit is a person doesn't develop **other methods** to reduce anxiety. Having several ways to manage emotions, as the situation dictates is empowering. When I met Glenda, she did not have even one method, except to puff her lungs with nicotine, on the path to emphysema oblivion.

The unconscious mind stores within, definitions of what is good and bad. Your interpretation of stress may be quite different to the next person. Sometimes your beliefs are an advantage whereas other times, for no apparent reason you are triggered into anxiety. In this next example I talk with Glenda about an anxious episode she had.

The cause of anxiety is mostly unconscious (not in our awareness), so it is useful to become aware, then find a healing perspective. The goal is to lower thoughts of disaster and self-judgement, via higher minded thinking. In other words, 'thinking better thoughts to feel better.'

PHONE CALL #1 UNDERPANTS

As part of my quit cigarettes program, I offer a lifetime guarantee. This means we work together until there is confidence to remain a non-smoker. Glenda utilised 2 support phone calls in the first week. Anxiety was high and she felt helpless. She believed that everything would fall apart, saying, "There must be something wrong with me."

I reassured that her body was going through a transformation and she would be okay. If Glenda's feelings could be encapsulated in one word, it would be overwhelmed. On the first phone call, she told me that anxiety was heightened. I asked, "What happened?"

Her property is in an isolated area, with the mailbox 100 metres from the house, down by the roadside. Wearing a light summer dress she made her way to check if any letters had arrived. Suddenly a gust of wind blew Glenda's dress over her head, exposing underpants to a car driving by, she didn't recognise.

She was mortified that someone could have seen her undies and hurried back inside the house. What was probably interesting to the people in the car, was anything but for Glenda. She was stuck with dead end beliefs and questions. "It's terrible. Why did this happen to me? How could I let this happen?"

Glenda believed that the event was so terrible, she would be unable to walk on her own property again and was too anxious to visit the shopping centre, due to the risk of being recognised. Her interpretation was doom and gloom. This seemed to be something she was very familiar with. I was determined that she could use this as a healing opportunity.

If I don't re-define my circumstances, I will be stuck with my unconscious mind's definition by default.

The event involving her, and the car, did happen. That is solid but Glenda could find a little flexibility in her perspective. I said, "I'm hearing that you have given this incident a meaning. Something terrible has happened and it's wrong and embarrassing that people driving by, saw your underpants."

Me: "I want you to consider that in future your interpretation of this situation can be different. You will be able to look back with a higher perspective. You are not stuck with this anxiety. The meaning of this event is something you can choose.

Let's start with the people in the car. The strangers passing by the mailbox were unknown to you, so probably not local. The odds of seeing them again are very slim and in any case the dress was over your head, so they may not have seen your face.

Nothing bad happened to the strangers, they were probably surprised and have a story to talk about while driving. Nothing bad happened to you. You were and are completely uninjured. It's not your fault a gust of wind blew, at that exact moment. You have done nothing wrong, and your body is the most natural thing there is."

I pause and sense she is hopeful.

"By the way Glenda, do you have grandkids?"

Glenda: "Yes, 2 of them."

Me: "You were unharmed and made someone's day driving past your house who would have never expected to see what they did. That's interesting right? Wouldn't the grandkids find it amazing if grandma was not the fortress of solitude they know you to be. You can be fun and vulnerable, by claiming this story.

When you own the story, it doesn't own you. That is power. Artists do this, with paintings, music, comedy, movies and poetry. You can choose the meaning. If you find 'comedy' in your 'tragedy,' you bring lightness to yourself and other people. Whether you tell the story or not is up to you.

Life is a joke. Life is a learning experience. Life is terrible. Life is a waste. Life is about love, family and service. Life is about knowledge and contribution. These are all beliefs people have. None of them are absolute truth. You can choose how you want to live. It's time now to release the 'everything is terrible' story and try a new one."

I ask Glenda to say this next paragraph with me. Speaking a new idea out loud creates more neural connections than reading and listening alone.

Together: "Anxiety says things are bad and wrong. We say, life is not only good or bad, there is plenty of room in between to move around and breathe freely."

Me: "Anxiety doesn't let us breathe. It tightens the chest and restricts the mind. It is not a bad thing that happened. You are okay and everybody involved is safe. Outside of that, what things mean are choices you can make. What do you think about that?"

Glenda: "It could be funny."

Glenda: "Maybe I could claim this story as an opportunity for growth."

Glenda was unstuck from the situation being totally bad, to acknowledging it could be something else. Her mind was open to new, useful ways of thinking. We didn't avoid what happened but explored healing possibilities. Having a variety of interpretations gives the mind flexibility. Refer to the Alternate Meaning Technique in the last chapter.

PHONE CALL #2 MEDITATION

A few days later we chatted again. Glenda mentioned that she had tried the breathing technique I recommended at her original appointment. I asked what effect this had on her emotions.

She replied, "It didn't calm me down. I'm just so anxious." Glenda had health issues that needed attention, didn't feel physically safe and was fearful of her lung illness worsening.

I was curious to find out what occurred because the equal breathing technique, done for 20 minutes has a very high success rate in calming physiology. Was her physical tension too high for it to work? What happened in this particular case?

Glenda performed equal breathing while wearing a towel. While upstanding, she made intense eye contact with herself in the mirror. I imagined what it must have felt like; tense and trying to force relaxation. I assured her that it would work better with changes.

Me: "Your effort is admirable. Let's make sure the technique is right for you. This breathing process is designed to reacquaint you with the parasympathetic nervous system. Perhaps wearing comfortable clothing, while sitting and eyes closed would allow relaxation. The more you practice meditation for calmness, the more effective it will become."

Additional relaxation tip: For your first 10 ten breaths in meditation, exhale with an audible sigh of release. Let the tension float away. When breathing out say "aaahhhhhhhhhh… ooohhhhhhhhhh." Be aware that letting go of tension this way could result in an emotional release. Have some tissues nearby, just in case.

MEDITATION

Meditation can be done simply, by following these steps:

- Sit comfortably
- Eyes closed
- Focus attention on your breathing
- Allow any thoughts to just be (not avoided or resisted)
- Complete your meditation for 20 minutes

In meditation we are prioritising the present moment, over all else. Our body and mind can learn that it is okay to slow down. Meditation is not a doing activity. It is a 'being' process. Make the decision that meditating is more important than stimulation by work and technology?

If general stress is heightened, it is worth being still for 20 minutes, twice daily. When first awakened in the morning and just before bed are good opportunities for meditation. A safe and distraction-free environment is ideal. An indoor location is preferred over the outdoors, which can be affected by weather.

In meditation you are aware yet not overstimulated.

There is a purpose for the meditation being 20 minutes. This is the length of time it takes for the body to relax at a deeper level. You might experience peace during meditation. Other times you might have sensations of tension. This can happen due to slowing down enough, to actually notice how we are feeling.

Select audio tracks, instead of a noisy alarm to conclude meditation. I find Stuart Jones relaxation/massage music to be excellent. When the song ends, you know you are finished. It may be better to use an instrumental soundtrack rather than a song with lyrics.

We aren't trying to escape feelings during meditation, instead we become present and breathe through them. This is self-regulation. With practice, a gap will form in your mind. The space between your thoughts increases. Emotional volatility will settle down.

Observe thoughts, say thank you and return focus to meditation.

Whilst meditating you might have a distracting thought. You can observe it for a moment, thank the thought for visiting and return focus to your breathing technique. A guilty thought might come along later on, "I wish I hadn't screwed that up." You can observe for a moment, thank it for visiting and return focus to your breathing technique.

In the initial stages of meditation, you might be fidgety or itchy. That's okay. Spend a few minutes getting these out of the way. Shuffle around to find a comfy position, scratch if necessary, then place full awareness onto your inhale and exhale.

Affirmation: "In this present moment I am completely okay. I accept myself as I am now."

ACCEPTANCE OF THOUGHTS AND SELF

Meditation teaches us that our imagination does not require reaction. Thoughts can just be. We can observe an idea in our mind and not interact. Most times there will be thoughts in meditation however there is no need to resist them. You can softly prioritise breathing, parallel with your thoughts.

Judgemental thinking will be observed, thanked and that's all. There could be tension in your body when these thoughts surface. With meditation, you are training your mind to be non-reactive to these sensations and thus over time unwanted feelings settle into the background.

You can tell unhelpful thoughts that you will be occupied for the next 20 minutes. "I am not interacting today. Thank you."

Think of meditation as an opportunity to be yourself. You aren't expected to do anything, just being as you are. By being you, you are practicing self-acceptance in the present moment. There is no longer a war with thoughts and anxiety. You have stopped fighting and controlling, and so the emotional energy will be less.

Saying thank you to an unhelpful thought is healing.

I used to become agitated during meditation. My mind would start counting breaths. I tried to refocus. It felt like the counting urge was getting in the way of my calm. After several meditations with tension, I decided to count breaths by choice (deliberately) and the stress dropped away. Counting actually gave my mind a single thing to focus on, this helped meditation.

If anxious thoughts visit and you observe in non-reaction, that is progress. When you simply observe, your brain makes vital healing connections, habitually and hormonally. Practicing observation of thoughts gives your mind the possibility to do it again. Do it several times and non-reaction becomes a healthy habit, that occurs automatically.

EQUAL BREATHING

In addition to breathing in meditation, some may enjoy a visual process. You can draw a square in your mind with eyes closed. With this technique draw 1 line of the square for each of the four steps.

Step 1) Inhale for 4 seconds
Step 2) Hold the breath for 4 seconds
Step 3) Exhale for 4 seconds
Step 4) Pause between breaths for 4 seconds

On the inhale, draw a straight line from left to right. While holding the breath, draw a line from top to bottom. On the exhale, draw a line from right to left. When pausing, draw a line from the bottom, upwards thus completing your square.

This process of drawing a square, can be good if you have trouble 'doing nothing.' Be sure to let your face muscles, shoulders, hands and feet soften as you meditate. Consider meditation as part of your regular lifestyle, for long-term results. Even if it is not perfect you are still supporting your body and mind toward healing, which is worthwhile.

MINDFULNESS CONCLUSION

Where am I currently on my list of things to do? Between work, family, house maintenance, cleaning, cooking, watching mobile phone content and other obligations, where is self-nurturing? Breathing and self-talk are with me everywhere I go. This means mindfulness is always within reach. We can breathe and think nicely.

Is it psychologically healthy to talk to myself? Yes, internal communication is simply a normal mind function. Self-talk already happens and by directing it, you are taking control of the process. I am suggesting that you actively instruct your mind to work for you.

Talk with your subconscious mind every day. Anxious self-talk includes what ifs, minimisations and exaggerations. With a mindfulness pattern you direct thinking to **higher ideas and truth**. Thinking can be optimistic and grateful. Enough empowering, mindful thoughts and your physiology responds with relief and ease.

Are there other ways to be mindful? Journalling your thoughts in a notebook is effective. By writing things down, you get them 'out of your head.' Ruminating about every little thing won't be necessary because writing gives your thoughts physical expression, on the page. When journalling I suggest writing down what happens each day and gratitude for your blessings.

SUBCONSCIOUS HEALING INSTRUCTION

"Anxiety thank you. YOU can relax now. You have been a protector, harsh judger, catastrophiser and shamer of mine for many years but, being on high alert all the time is not working. We're not fighting anymore. I have laid down my weapons and well, you never had any to begin with. Only my reactions to you had power and I don't believe your imaginations anymore. I decide what I'm going to think and feel today. My higher mind will be making the major decisions from now on. Just as a parent does not permit certain behaviours from their child, I absolutely will no longer allow self-judgement and delusions.

I believe in truth, on the healing journey. I believe in knowledge and self-acceptance. My learning curve is ongoing and I like that. I am in no rush. I am a happy learner, because that's where I get better. Whew, what a relief to know my thoughts can just be there and I don't have to control them. Hey, anxiety I hope you heard all that. There is nothing for you to do. A request for my mind, whisper to me anything useful and real. I will listen to this. I'm ensuring my own safety now. I am learning about my wants, needs and alignment and expressing to others. I am conscious of thoughts and stay calm. Normal physical sensations will come and leave my body. My mind is in control of my body. I am present. I observe myself in calmness. I am safe. I am healing. I've got this."

Affirmation: "My brain is my friend."

THE POWER OF INTENTION

MY INTENTIONS

I had written on my Vision Wall for years, that I wanted free massages. I was told that "what I think about, and thank about, I will bring about." I was very grateful for every paid massage I bought and after a few years the strangest thing happened. One day a lady called, who wanted me to teach her Hypnotherapy.

I agreed to share about Hypnotherapy and business, in exchange for massage therapy. She looked after my shoulder strains from a previous injury and I encouraged her in business.

Upon arrival there were 5 steps outside that led to a balcony. The area was overgrown with plants and vines snaking up the outside walls. There appeared to be more vegetation than house. Inside the front door was a long hallway. Down the end I could see stacked boxes and furniture cluttering the space.

I spotted a picture up on the far wall of a naked lady. Before I could think much about it, I was ushered into the room immediately on my left, just after the entrance. "Take off your clothes," she instructed. "For massage."

I was relieved for a moment, then concerned! In front of me

was a massage table, with ropes either side. I thought I had entered some kind of sex room and didn't want to be tied up and used for who knows what! I thought for a moment. Probably unlikely. That doesn't happen, does it? And what about the naked picture in the other room? The portrait was of her younger self.

I didn't sense any danger and could always say no if things – go south. The massage was very good (and professional). It turns out ropes were for stretching the body. After treatment, we went past the living room to the kitchen. There was a small, square space, with a tiny fold up table in the centre.

I was ushered to sit on the single chair at the table, with all the hospitality that could be expected at a restaurant. In front of me was a plate, covered with another plate. She revealed a big meal of rice, vegetables and chicken. "Wow," I said. My comment was as much about the gesture, as about the amount of food. "Eat up," she said. "I'll try," I replied.

I ate and we chatted about hypnotherapy, business and her journey. I looked forward to it each week. We developed a friendship. Unusual and strange circumstances like this suit my personality. It's interesting to me what might happen next, like twists and turns in a movie.

The friendship ended suddenly and in a sad way. A project we worked on fizzled out and she contracted a rare illness that resulted in her being bed ridden. She didn't want me to visit again, probably out of pride, possibly embarrassed to be seen in a weakened state. I called several times to check-in.

The unfortunate ending aside, what occurred was exactly what I'd intended. Hypnotherapy, business, friendship, food and massage therapy were 5 things I 'thought about' and 'thanked about' regularly. Not long after I met my fiancé. She is a remedial massage therapist and English teacher, who is intelligent, funny, cooks delicious food, brilliantly edits my books and lights up my world.

I believe the people in our lives, in this present moment are aligned with who we are and what we think about most often. For a long while I didn't know where friends would come from or believe that I would ever find a new partner.

I got really honest about what I wanted. With a small group of friends, I voiced and wrote down all the traits desirable to me in a partner. Given the choice with no limitations, "What do I most want in a relationship?"

Having certainty with what I intended gave me peace. I know I've done the work that allows more blessings to arrive, without the guilt. When she turned up, I was ready for the opportunity because I knew who and what I wanted.

Intention setting has a compounding effect. The more you do it the better it works. You start to see opportunities, not previously noticed. People become more helpful. Job offers fall in your lap. Certain people catch your eye and are drawn to you. By focusing on what you want, you subconsciously attract what is aligned.

LYNDA'S TRICKS

Lynda is a friend I have learnt a great deal from. I interviewed her about the journey she took to become a transformation coach. Growing up, an alcoholic mother made life very difficult. She described a time when there was so much restriction, although Lynda desired to feel joyful every day. Later, she worked for a long time in her husband's business and raised children.

Life during this time was okay but not by her design. Work was fine and family duties completed but these were roles she slipped into by default. Something felt missing in her soul. When she decided to pursue her dreams, it wasn't received well at first. Her husband would have to find a new employee and *pay them* a wage. Her kids would have to take on more responsibility too.

Lynda: "I started by being grateful for all the abundance in my life presently. With this attitude of gratitude, I appreciated what was already there and started attracting more blessings. I am appreciative for all that I have and all that I will experience. There is enough good to go around for everyone."

Lynda: "There is joy, freedom and abundance in my past, present and future."

It was interesting to me how she is grateful for future blessings. She's committed to a vision, so it appears more often. She is really making the most of the power of intention here. **Being thankful for things you haven't yet experienced, is manifestation work at its finest.**

Lynda aligns her thoughts with what she wants. She practices dozens of times every day. An intention practiced over and over will create reality. Her car and clothes feel joyful. She walks, talks and dresses in a way that makes her feel this way. I could hear the sincerity with which she spoke. This is how Lynda lives.

The mind cannot help but be focused on blessings when you think about it so much. In our interview I wanted to go deeper. What happens when life just sucks?

Me: "Okay, some people are more challenging than others. What about when you encounter conflict and family arguments?"

Lynda: "A little trick I use, is to say to myself, this person is having an interesting experience. I wonder what is affecting their state of mind. I get curious about what beliefs are causing their outburst. If someone is angry, I assume at some level they are needing love."

Me: "Why does that work for you?"

Lynda: "Because curiosity acts as an intervention away from reactive anger. It leads me to be more understanding about their circumstances. When people feel understood it dissolves a lot of hurt feelings. Two or more angry people doesn't fit in with a joyful intention, so this tactic gets me back there quicker. I'm not perfect by any means but curiosity works most times to calm all involved."

Me: "What about when you wake up feeling uninspired? Are there times you don't care or your mood is flat?"

Lynda chuckled to herself in a practiced way and said: "That used to happen a lot. There was a fog of mediocrity. I was going through the motions in my old life. What I do now if I can't cause uplifting feelings in myself, is to do it for others. Sure, I can feel flat sometimes, so I'll give abundance to those around me."

Me: "What do you mean by giving abundance to others?"

Lynda: "That's easy. I buy the person's beverage in front of me at a coffee shop. I stop to help people who look like they need it. I pass along things that I love to family, friends and strangers. I compliment people and talk to them about gratitude. I teach abundance as a topic in my coaching courses."

Lynda: "The number of times I've seen a roomful of people shift their negative attitude, with a few minutes of joyful energy, is amazing."

I observed in Lynda that she actively manages her mind. When challenge happens, she intervenes with a **mindful thought process**. Deciding that family is 'interesting' and not horrible is a choice she makes. A 'joyful intention' around uptight strangers, is a deliberate manifestation tool.

Lynda intends joy, abundance and freedom whether it seems likely to occur or not. It's a creation process. This is not reacting to reality however, **this is causing reality.** I could smile when interacting with a cashier. I could compliment more. I could think about joy, freedom and abundance. Lynda does it.

A note on Lynda's trick of spreading joy. She is not trying to uplift others at the expense of her own needs. For decades she did that and it was unknown how to live an abundant life. It wasn't even in her realm of possibility. She wants to show people that it is possible to feel really good most of the time. We are here for one-another. There is enough good to share around. This re-enforces the empowering beliefs in herself.

Her intention is very achievable because it is integrated into lifestyle. There are several opportunities each day to feel joyful, abundant and free. She can give it to herself and to others. Why not try one or more of the following yourself, over the next week?

- A gratitude ritual to focus on blessings
- Aligning words, actions and lifestyle with joy
- A curious intention around challenging people
- Being the change you want to see in the world
- Choose an intention that is healing

When reading these stories about intention it is reasonable to think that it doesn't work or some people are lucky. In order to make significant change, a strong intention always lies behind one's success. I have met people who got themselves out of the poverty cycle, which took years, or like Laura who we'll read about next, broke an anxiety pattern in 1 hour.

CAUSATION

"It is like planting a seed in the ground. It is not necessarily true at the moment but it is something you want to have be true. So, you put the seed in and expect it to grow."
Louise Hay

The phrase "fake it until you make it" gets used a lot in relation to goal setting. Being fake is not recommended but embodying something you want to be real is useful. Trying out a new thought pattern is different. This does mean fake. We embody a new way of being until it becomes integrated.

At first trying something new doesn't feel true. If I am on one side of the river but want to be over the other side, I take the bridge to get across. While you are intention setting see yourself as crossing over from the old to the new. Keep focused on where you are headed.

"Thinking better thoughts, causes better results."

In order to cross the river we need a bridge. That bridge might be strong or could be a bit rickety, like in Indiana Jones and The Temple of Doom. In any case best to put one foot in front of the other. I will cross this gap in my mind. There will be many rivers and bridges in our lifetime.

Anxiety says there is no way. Empowerment says, I am already working on a way and focused on the end result. If you are reading this book you are a human being and as such, you have encountered many challenges and are still persevering. You have strength to change the content of your mind and thus the conditions of your life for the better.

LAURA'S PICNIC

Laura found herself living life on high alert. She was a personal trainer and mother to a 2-year-old girl. Nothing terribly bad had happened but anxiety was steadily increasing. "I'm anxious while running, shopping, seeing friends and going out to dinner. All these normal activities used to be fine but now I dread them. If plans change the panic gets even worse."

I could relate to anxiety about plan changes. I used to pre-think my social interactions in a way that was like treading water. I had to keep my head up to survive. Things must happen how I want them to. The event must be at the original time and place. One small difference to the schedule and I was drowning.

When setting an intention, make it flexible and attainable. For example, in my relationship, a useful intention is to listen well. This is achievable. A rigid goal would be something like, I intend for the relationship to be perfect, all the time.

A flexible intention for what you want, is more desirable than rigid perfection. Flexibility allows life to unfold and can include enjoyment. Focus on what you want, stated in the affirmative. You can create an intention that allows plenty of opportunity to come true.

Laura had very high anxiety, self-rated at 9/10 intensity. We chatted about how she could use intention to see the dreaded event (visiting friends) going well. Laura was accustomed to anxiousness and using rigid rules, to control everything. Usually nothing bad happens, but it sure does feel like it will.

Me: "The location, timing and people don't need to be perfect. We know that trying to control every detail leads to overwhelm. Enjoyment need not be micro-managed out of what can be a wonderful day for you and family. Let's add a little intention for a good time."

Me: "Can you describe a terrific picnic with your friends? What are all the best things that can happen? The purpose is to know exactly what you want. This will help your subconscious mind think and feel optimistic when the time comes. Good things *can* happen. It activates enthusiasm in the body and mind. It can allow hope in the heart."

Laura: "I can imagine turning up, greeting friends with warm hugs, smiling and seeing others return that smile. I will feel the pleasant weather on my skin. I will help others have a good time too, with fun and laughter. I can see my daughter running around and I'm relaxing."

Me: "That's right. The anxiety was a future imagination. A series of thoughts about things not going well. You have now created this new collection of thoughts, feelings and images in your mind. Is that visualisation right for you?"

Laura: "Yes. It feels right, I usually like seeing friends as long as the worry is not there. Also, I am allowing myself the freedom to leave at any time I choose."

Me: "Is there anything you would add or take away from this picture."

Laura: "It's good. I am just excited to turn up tomorrow."

Me: "Is the intention achievable and feels good for your mind and body?"

Laura: "Yes."

The freedom to leave at any time felt like safety. Her mind and body softened in front of me. When we embody freedom of choice, it is healing. You can go where you want for 10 minutes, 5 hours, however long. Release the idea of trying to please everybody else, infinitely. Live life on your terms.

With no self-imposed rules bogging her down, natural motivation to socialise was returning. Events do not have to happen a certain way and several good things can take place.

We also added a meditation/breathing technique that reduces emotional energy. I recommended she use it sometime before socialising. If the picnic is at 10:00am, then around 8:00am meditate for 10-20 minutes. Visualise the outcome you want, feel the sunshine and the hugs. Being generally relaxed before an event means lower potential for anxiety, later in the day.

If we are very used to imagining the worst happening, then it's worth giving our mind another picture. A better, brighter and more beautiful picture to work with.

Can my thoughts really change how I feel? They do every single day. I'm going to have a crap day at the park, get scared and want to leave immediately when arriving. Or I am going to have a lovely day at the park. I'm looking forward to friends, food and my daughter having a fun time. I can leave whenever I choose to.

Regardless of what does happen, there are no longer rigid rules fuelling anxiety. She will hug her friends. There are multiple opportunities to have fun with her daughter, friends and other people at the park. There is a high probability of success because the outcomes are simple, heart-felt and easy to achieve.

Like Lynda (from our last story), if you intend to make someone else's day, that gives us a greater feeling too. It's not a rule to follow. It is opportunity you can open up to. Like a flower happy to receive the sunrise.

Some keys for setting an intention:

- Include safety
- Relaxed breathing before the event
- Picturing the desired outcome
- Spreading enjoyment to others
- See intention setting as an opportunity

We had the beginnings of a plan for anxiety relief. Results were better than expected. Laura got back to me a few days later and didn't need a second appointment. She felt excited and light, for the first time in years. I planned to share additional tools but it was not needed. The visualisation was readily accepted by body and mind, and she felt optimistic.

I received this feedback from Laura:

"I just wanted to say thank you from the bottom of my heart… I took your advice and relinquished control to an extent. My daughter asked to go for a bike ride today… normally, with my anxiety I would have had to plan that. Today I practiced the breathing techniques you taught me, packed the car and went. I didn't panic once.

On the way back to the car was a true test. She asked to go to the park. I never EVER take her on Saturdays. Way too many kids and people, which is sure to send me into a meltdown… Well today, I did it!! We put the bike away and went to play with 20 or so other people there. Not one smidgen of anxiety!! So thank you, thank you, thank you. You helped make me make my daughter's day!"

DESTRESS OPTIONS

Do you believe that no matter how much stress, we should be unaffected? Do you believe that powering on indefinitely with high stress is achievable? Inevitably we use physical and emotional energy to solve problems but how much can our nervous system handle?

We want to take care of stress without succumbing to burnout, collapse or full-blown addiction to escape our reality. Periodically it is worth stepping back from your daily workload, to see what stress reduction options are available. If you have high stress at present, here is an opportunity to be strategic. We want to be effective (get workload completed) yet also reduce stress on the mind and body.

Think about whatever team sport you are most familiar with, whether it be football, basketball or something else. There is a teammate being well marked by the defence. Pass to this player and the ball will be lost. You pivot, facing a new direction where there are 2 players clearly in the open. Both are unmarked and one of them is in position to score.

An empowered mind is still aware of the poor option but does a pivot manoeuvre. A change of direction means better results are more likely. The blocked path exists but so do options B and C.

It is not empowering to focus on the blocked path. That's what anxiety does. The mind focuses on "It is bad, it is wrong, it will last forever." In sport the players cannot spend 6 hours staring at the blocked path. That just doesn't happen. Instead, they observe their environment, looking for the best possible option.

SUBSTITUTE NEGATIVE FOCUS, FOR THE PIVOT APPROACH

You can tell your mind: "Let's focus on the open path. I've got this now. If you (anxiety) have any useful suggestions, speak now otherwise be silent. It is time for a new direction. I will not spend my life focused on the blocked path while there is something I can do about it."

When we see a negative situation, we must remind ourselves this is not the whole story. Like a player we can't pass the ball to, this is simply one blocked avenue. A pivot enables you to quickly choose a more favourable path. Passing to the teammate who is in the open and could score, is the best option.

There is a video of Lionel Messi scanning the field before receiving the ball. He is aware of the positions of his nearest teammates and depending on what the defence does, he can pivot one direction or another, knowing he has passing options. He can also run the ball himself and back his abilities, when the time calls for it.

The nature of sport is forward motion. You observe, change direction and act. You can speed up your pivot. Rather than seeing only the problem for hours on end, encourage your mind to ask, "What options do I have now? Which path is open for me?"

But what if it's hard to pinpoint the cause? What if I'm stressed by everything?

On the path of healing your anxiety there will be things that work and don't work. It's forward motion we are focused on now. While on this worthwhile journey expect hurdles along the way. This is not cause to give up on our goals and dreams. I know problems will turn up sometimes. Best I can, I'll look for a healing action or better perspective. Move on to the next best option that creates a healing possibility.

Taking actions give you feedback. Thinking about action gives nothing.

To progress in healing use 1 of these 5 strategies. Stress does impact us. We all have a threshold of what we can reasonably handle. It is worth being honest when we are struggling. Here are 5 ways we can lower stress caused by unresolved problems and heavy workload.

STRATEGY 1 RESOLVE THE PROBLEM

Solving the problem behind the stress is an ideal strategy to use. For example, if there is financial stress and business takes off, providing surplus cash, the pressure is less. In another example, when there is a marriage argument, then both parties reach agreement, the problem is solved. The solution has to be genuinely acceptable for both people.

If you are stressed about money, work on finances. If stressed about your relationship, work on your relationship. If stressed about health issues, work on improving nutrition and following up with your health-care team. Can the problem be solved by addressing the issue at hand?

MATTHEW'S FINANCES (RESOLVE THE PROBLEM)

In 2016 I co-facilitated an online program for Dads. One of the men had been stressed for several years about his financial situation. It became a habit to ignore the problem, which snowballed into a $100,000 tax debt.

Matthew was using the avoidance pattern. Out of sight, out of mind. But... it wasn't out of mind. His internal dialogue was nagging at him, "Stop avoiding will you, just get it over and done with!" I reflected back his self-talk. "Stress is communicating that procrastination is not working. Corrective action is needed, so that is the best path to take."

Me: "This stress is feedback that finances need your attention. You might not feel great about yourself, acknowledging debt that has grown but when you act, you will start to feel better fairly quickly. Stress challenges us to solve problems and rewards with relief and pride."

Matthew made inquiries to find out the exact amount he was liable and made a surprising discovery. The debt was $40,000 less than he believed. He was willing to work on a $100,000 debt, so the $59,200 figure seemed like a piece of cake in comparison. He said, "Even if the figure had been higher, knowing the truth was relieving."

He was out of his 'anxious cave' and actually feeling excited. Small achievements generate enthusiasm for men and women alike. It's a healthy reward. The debt was still a burden he had to tackle however it felt good to be back in the game.

This situation was resolved quickly for Matthew once he pivoted. It took just 2 phone calls with his Accountant and the Australian Tax Office, for everything to be set up. The debt repayments would commence on a fortnightly basis, at an amount he could afford and there was no more stress. He knows exactly how long it will take to be debt-free and this certainty relieved him.

Resolving this specific stress created outcomes that he hadn't expected. At the conclusion of my time working with Matthew he stopped drinking (his preferred escapism). Was exercising regularly, lost several kilos and had finances accounted for. When a problem has been avoided for a long time, it is worth working on the issue directly. Little by little, day by day, it will get done.

Matthew pivoted from the alcohol avoidance ritual to the 'just do it' ritual.

STRATEGY 2 DISTANCE FROM STRESS

If there is something that makes you incredibly stressed, consider removing yourself from that situation. Overwhelm may be feedback that a person, job or situation is not for you. Creating distance could be short, like a break or holiday. In other circumstances, removing yourself from the stress entirely is appropriate.

For a bullying example, if boundary setting is not helping, then leaving this dangerous and unhealthy situation could be the best option. Is there a place, activity, or person you can remove yourself from? Is a pivot to more favourable circumstances needed?

CHRISTINE'S MANAGER (DISTANCE FROM STRESS)

Christine had taken several months of leave, due to stress. During this time, she didn't work and was dedicated to improving mental health. Two issues she wanted to resolve were emotional eating and weight gain. Meals were inconsistent, often skipping breakfast and lunch. When emotional, she consumed sugar close to bedtime.

In the week following her visit to my clinic, she made better food choices and was doing it without needing to use willpower. Christine felt happy and confident. Stress overall was lower and she, "Didn't even feel like eating sugar."

The first week after treatment can often be excellent yet it is also worth preparing for potential stresses. I asked if there was a scenario in the future where she might be concerned of reverting to emotional eating.

Was there a challenge she needed to prepare for? What had triggered emotional eating before? I asked these questions for the purpose of building her resilience. Success does not happen with only positive thinking and hope. A solid mental health plan buffers against future challenges.

Being aware of her biggest trigger, meant she would be confident dealing with it in the future. If there is a recurrence of stress, she will then be mindful to take a healing action.

She told me details of her work situation before taking a leave of absence. Christine was a co-ordinator in a government department and carried a lot of responsibility. Most of the time she loved it, thriving on achieving targets, excellence and having an organised workplace.

Recently there had been personnel changes. The new bunch of workmates were lazy, gossiped about team members and the manager didn't care about performance. The new supervisor had actually asked that she lower her work ethic.

After a few more questions it was revealed that she struggled working alongside leaders with low standards. "I get anxious and angry." However, with leaders that encouraged meeting targets and showed appreciation, she thrived.

A high-quality manager who shows appreciation goes a long way. Her breakthrough question was

"How were your stress levels and eating patterns whilst working with a high-quality manager?"

Christine replied: "I had very little stress and ate minimal sugar."

At that moment she realised the source of stress was related to the management structure above her. When there is poor leadership at work, stress and comfort eating increase. She looked forward to working again, under a manager or company that was professional; where she could make a difference?

A comfort eating ritual had taken the place of a fulfilling work ritual.

Me: "Would you be confident eating well when your work is enjoyable and fulfilling?"

Christine's energy changed as her brain connected the dots and at the end of those dots was a healing possibility. Distance from inept managers significantly lowered Christine's stress. That's why she needed a break. "When work is rewarding, I don't really have food problems or weight gain."

When Christine was denied rewarding work, she used sugar to stimulate the dopamine centre of her brain. It is reasonably common for those lacking work fulfillment to struggle with compulsions. Those who are achieving goals that are meaningful to them, have far less tendency to addiction and relapse.

Lacking in fulfillment means we are more likely to create artificial reward, through compulsions and addictions. Higher levels of sugar, drug use, medication, alcohol, cigarettes and gambling could be overcompensating for lesser purpose and passion in life.

Back to Christine. Changing eating habits are easier because she knows the main trigger for sugar cravings which was used for stress relief and reward. Now she is aware that she desires excellence at work and distance from low-quality managers.

Sugar cravings are not about sugar, it's about what the sugar is being used for. If Christine does enter a situation of high stress again, she has options now. Leave and seek employment that is fulfilling. Stay in the job short-term and use other ways to release stress. Her heightened awareness tells her now, "I am desiring fulfillment. I am not hungry for sugar!"

When the real reason for binge eating and comfort eating is dealt with, you will feel completely in control. Awareness questions: If you regularly crave sweets, where are you missing sweetness in life? Do I need space from a challenging person, job or situation?

STRATEGY 3 DELEGATING STRESS

Delegating unwanted and time-consuming tasks, is great for business and families. Your taxes, cleaning, food delivery, completing paperwork and child minding are possible examples of things that can be delegated.

A little money can be used to delegate your stress. Tasks that are undesirable to you, may be quite acceptable for someone else for a fee. Delegation does not need to include financial exchange either. Agreements can be made, to undertake tasks that you are suited to. A life that is aligned, means people and activities are matched to who they are.

MONICA'S BATH (DELEGATING STRESS)

Monica visited my office in 2015. She was a single mother to 3 children, aged 12, 10 and 8. As I often do, I asked about the ways she currently nurtures herself. She revealed one of the most creative self-care rituals I have heard.

Monica has enjoyed an hour-long bath, every Sunday for the last 15 months. She doesn't get a babysitter for the kids but has organised something unique. While she gets an hour of peace, soaking in the tub, the 3 children tidy the entire house. Monica hasn't missed a single Sunday, in case the routine stops and a good thing is lost.

Not only does Monica nurture herself for 1 hour, the kids clean house at the same time.

Delegating household tasks became possible due to planning and genuinely getting the kids on board. The children picked their preferred chores from a list of options, so they weren't stuck with something they absolutely hated.

Knocking on the bathroom door was only allowed for a proper emergency. Not because, "Sally stole my Baby Yoda teddy bear." or whatever. The house was cleaned with varying degrees of quality.

"Why do I deserve relaxation time when others have it worse than me? Am I bad for working the kids like this?" Monica shared doubts and guilt with friends about this bath time ritual. It felt wrong and she hadn't heard of anyone else doing this. After chatting with other parents, they reassured her to enjoy it!

She finished each bath replenished and calm of mind. Monica became more patient at home and work. There were benefits to her children too, such as being responsible and working as a team to achieve a goal. Not to mention, a relaxed Mum is good for everybody.

I love this on many levels. There's the creativity of combining self-care and the children being helpful. The delegation of house duties meant they weren't just mess makers but also cleaners too. The delegation of chores included input and choice from the kids.

- She believed it could work and it did

- The children show care for their mother, not just the other way round
- They learn that looking after yourself as a parent is acceptable by watching Mum do it
- Through her example the children are more likely to grow into adults who nurture themselves too

STRATEGY 4 SUPPORT BODY WITH LIFESTYLE

When addressing stress, you can support yourself with lifestyle. Eating quality food and exercise have a big impact on improving emotional state. Other nurturing activities include; immersion in nature, swimming, yoga, rest, meditation, connection with people/animals and being gentle with yourself.

Some situations like health issues, renovating a house and caring for family, can't be resolved in one go. We need healthy lifestyle to support body and mind. This is a safe and reliable way to release pressure.

LILLIAN'S COLLAPSE (SUPPORT BODY WITH LIFESTYLE)

"I don't eat breakfast or lunch. When highly stressed I won't have a proper dinner either. I consume 8-10 coffees a day, it's virtually stopped being a stimulant through overuse. I can stay awake for 48-72 hours straight however will become unconscious without warning. This resulted in my driver's licence being cancelled, due to risk of me falling asleep behind the wheel."

Lillian and I chatted about her health and life. She was formerly a nurse and is now caring full-time for a husband and 2 children with special needs. Her husband returned from military service with PTSD. He has good days but mostly challenging days. Cigarettes were her go to lifestyle habit when she wanted a break.

In the absence of a functional destress ritual, smoking filled the void. "It's very quick and easy to do." Life was exclusively lived in the sympathetic nervous system (stress and stimulation), followed by collapse. Although I have consulted with many overwhelmed people, hers was most serious due to loss of consciousness.

Such was the extent of Lillian's stress and anxiety, her nervous system decided to shut down from time to time. Although cigarettes allow her a break from stressful situations, they don't provide any significant grounding or relaxation, that is sorely needed.

Cigarettes also suppress appetite, and less appetite means lower overall nutrition. Puffing on a smoke, is different from the deeper relief felt, activating your parasympathetic nervous system. Here is what you can practically do.

Ways to activate the parasympathetic nervous system PNS:

- 20 minutes of meditation
- A tai chi or yoga class
- Physically connecting with nature and animals
- Hypnotherapy treatment

How the sympathetic nervous system SNS activates:

- Work excessively without breaks
- Avoid solving problems, turn to sugar, smoking and caffeine instead
- Have poor eating and sleep habits
- Be too focused on the past or future

Because Lillian's physiology was so extreme (high stress followed by unconsciousness), support through lifestyle was critical. Our body can only handle so much pressure, so it is important to lower overall stress levels. My suggestion was to incorporate rest that activates the PNS, for 20 minutes, twice per day.

Me: "Spontaneous collapse is a risk to safety, so I suggest using lifestyle to support your body and mind. Dedicating 40 minutes total per day to properly relaxing, will activate your parasympathetic nervous system. The purpose of a de-stress ritual is to lower your **baseline stress level** and therefore your anxiety.

Over time the body gets familiar relaxing without drugs, medication or collapse. Burnout is not the desired option with 2 kids and a partner to support. We need rest and space to process our human experience."

Lillian decided that short rituals wouldn't be enough. She started spending the whole day, once a week at a relative's property. She relaxed in a caravan on the farm, doing nothing or whatever she wanted.

Find opportunities to renew physical energy and mental clarity. You might like a little rest each day or a longer break once per week. Light meals full of vitamins are valuable. Fun and recreation may be the break needed to refresh your mind. The opportunity here is to acknowledge when your physiology has had enough and use healthy rituals to stabilise.

During this time food intake was increased. Lillian quit smoking and replaced most coffee with water. She took time out once per week in a natural farm setting. Lifestyle made a difference. The time you use to look after body and mind is well spent.

Chances are you are a service orientated person, taking care of family, putting others ahead of yourself. Are you the honourable one who cares deeply for others welfare, at the expense of your own? Do you take on extra shifts when asked? Work unpaid overtime? Say yes to friends' problems when there is already too much for you to do?

Are you the nurse, carer, teacher, worker or protector for those around you?

The low self-esteem character, who puts themselves last, secretly wants to scream in anger. Food, alcohol, cigarettes, drugs, phone scrolling and masturbation are used for stress relief or maybe all of these.

Saying no to other people's problems, is saying yes to yourself. If someone wants attention during your self-care ritual, you tell them you have an appointment. Tell your loved ones, you are unavailable during certain time periods. This is a healthy self-esteem action.

Here is how to do it. Choose 2x 20 minute periods prioritised for self-care. Book it in your diary, like it is a doctor's appointment. People keep their doctor's appointment, because they are necessary. Place a high importance on your recovery time.

Your relaxation ritual can be 20 minutes or longer.

STRATEGY 5 CHANGE YOUR PERSPECTIVE

What we focus on can make us feel stressed or blessed, stuck or progressing, worried or confident. My mind has worked against me so many times, usually because I did not want to experience pain. In therapy we open doors with questions. The better the questions, the greater the results.

Although most problems are temporary, some anxieties last a lifetime or even get passed down over generations, so it is very valuable to work on healing perspectives that can change this pattern. A healing perspective interrupts anxiety, providing thoughts that are safe, useful, realistic and help correct unhealthy patterns.

1. What is great about this problem?
2. What is true in this situation?
3. What am I grateful for right now?
4. Are there solutions available?
5. What would love do now?

DAVID'S VAPING (CHANGE YOUR PERSPECTIVE)

I assisted a gentleman who wanted to quit vaping. In case you are not aware a 'vape' is an electronic cigarette which is filled with various flavours and chemicals, like nicotine. David presented with difficulty sleeping, lethargy, stress at work and "wanting to improve well-being."

He worked in conjunction with insurance companies, and his team repaired damaged houses. He solved problems and made dozens of phone calls every day, to those in upper management and the team. When stressed, vaping was used as a coping mechanism.

Me: "David, what type of situations cause you stress?"

David: "When my team make a mistake, it adds to my workload. I have to fix the situation and explain to unhappy customers what went wrong and how long it will take to fix."

Me: "Are there 1 or 2 employees that mostly make mistakes or is it across the board?"

David: "Across the board."

Me: "How is accuracy of communication between upper management, yourself and staff?"

David: "It can be rushed sometimes, missing information."

Me: "In any team the number one confidence builder is knowledge. Does the team have all of the information they need? Are there times they don't know what to do? Is it possible to improve communication across the board, to minimise errors?"

I continued: "Clear instructions create accurate work and less errors. On complex projects a rushed phone call, means details could get missed or forgotten by staff. Misinterpretations could also occur. I wonder how much accuracy would increase if you combined a phone call with a step-by-step instructional email.

You could send an email to staff, outlining every single step for the job. This can include as much clarity and detail as needed. The email message could be saved as a template and used hundreds of times for future jobs, tweaked as needed and saving time in the long run. The purpose is to give very clear instructions so less things go wrong.

Think about setting up email templates for repeatable processes in tandem with a phone conversation. The work to prepare job templates will be a big time saver, once in place.

Seeing as there are so many errors, I'm wondering if communication is rushed and lacking detail. Take your time and verify that staff fully understand what to do. With a checklist, staff can review it as many times as needed. Easy to access information has a high chance of improving results.

They read the email and you give the team leader a call to verify they understand the importance of each step. Knowledge and support always make a project more successful. Do you feel these ideas could improve communication and therefore lessen mistakes?"

David: "Yes" while mind gazing into the future, picturing these new tactics in action.

Me: "When the job gets done right first time does that mean you can have more positive conversations with customers about work completed to their specifications?"

David: "Yes, it's less stress all around, saves time and improves our reputation."

Me: "When you are out smoking or vaping who is supporting the team?"

David: "For that 5 minutes, no one is. The problem is that's happening 15 or 20 times per day too."

Me: "So, the truth is you are falling behind with work and feeling unwell after vaping. You have avoided working to your potential as a leader and problem solver. No wonder you have been tired. Towards the end of our conversation, I asked if the following are true for him.

- Is there relief when jobs are completed properly?
- Does clear communication at work and home mean better results?
- Does being present rather than distracted mean better results?
- Would feeling healthy and energetic mean less stress?

We delved into just 2 of the questions at the start of this section. 'What is true?' and 'Are there solutions available?' This brought about a change of perspective; realising that vaping added to his stress, while other tactics (like clear communication) actually increased work standards, productivity, finances, presence, time, energy, self-pride and well-being.

The power of new perspective is not just thinking differently. It can shift our daily life. In David's case, a 20-year habit of smoking and vaping changed to, "I am really looking forward to being productive and getting things done right." He isn't avoiding stress at work, instead aiming for elite level communication so less problems occur in the first place.

Addiction always includes an anxious lie and it's really hard to perceive, when in the middle of it. His lie was this: I need smoking and vaping to relieve stress. The truth was avoidance CAUSED work stress, because he was not performing at his peak and ironically blaming others for not performing their roles too. The path of empowerment is doing his best at work, home and with health.

INTERVIEWS, GROUPS AND SOCIAL CONFIDENCE

I magine I am attending an interview and will meet the manager for the first time. For the sake of this story, their name is Steven. Steven runs a fashion company and is the gatekeeper to my dream job. We are yet to meet therefore I know nothing about what motivates and impresses him.

At the start of my interview imagine I say, "This is my dream, I want to be hired so much. I'll work any hours and come in on weekends. Whatever it takes." This strategy will not be very effective and could stop me getting the result I'm hoping for. I'll reveal how to show your enthusiasm just ahead.

If I throw myself at the interviewer, I'm actually asking them to decide my fate, with limited information to base their decision on. I am someone they don't know and questions will be on their mind. "What is wrong here? Are you desperate? How can you want it that much when the role, wage and details haven't been discussed yet?"

I have just set foot in the building, haven't met the team, supervisor, staff or customers. There is not enough information to assume this will fulfil my dream. I have already put the job on a pedestal, fantasising about how it will all be wonderful. Let's slow the process down. By listening first, I can gather information, then make a genuine impression.

INTERVIEW CONFIDENCE STEP 1: LISTEN AND LEARN

By initially listening, potential employer and employee gain confidence (caused by familiarity and knowledge). This is a relaxed approach to use in the interview process. We are not forcing a match however letting alignment unfold, by finding out about each other's personalities and values. When the time right, I can share my enthusiasm.

Attending a job interview wanting to impress people we haven't met and don't have rapport with is daunting. Trying to control what others think, may be working against us feeling the confidence we want. Ironically by letting go of control and focusing on the right things, we will be confident.

It makes sense that your first step should be a conversation. You are not under pressure. There will be information shared between the two of you, and you can perform a self-alignment check during the interview. Will this job fulfil my needs?

We need to have a slow and present conversation in an interview. Let Steven lead at first but ask questions to clarify what they said. In most cases a goal to be perfect can be *replaced* by a desire to learn and care. When it does come time to sell yourself, it will feel genuine and authentic.

If the interviewer happens to railroad you by asking what all your strengths are at the very start of the interview, reply with this. "I would love to learn more about the role, then I can share which of my skills are suited to your needs. What skills does your ideal candidate need?"

The interviewer may then go on to say they are a caring company (people focused) or sales driven (more money focused) or systems driven (accuracy focused). Based on what they say you can share your strengths that align with the job. You are ready for step 2 now.

INTERVIEW CONFIDENCE STEP 2: SHARE YOUR VALUE

What am I bringing to the table? I suggest writing a list of several qualities you will offer your new workplace. These can include general skills and those specific to the job. You have value (via your time, effort, skills and uniqueness). When writing your list, you can select traits below that describe work strengths and add your own:

- Hard worker
- Turns up on time
- Cares about people
- Have skills related to the job
- Experience in same or similar work
- Willingness to learn
- Creative
- Dress sense
- Attentive listener
- Problem solver
- Results focused
- Sales focused
- Details focused
- People focused
- Safety focused
- Leadership focused

When realising that you are valuable (after writing your list), you will not tolerate poor working conditions and a role that is unsuitable, nor uncaring attitudes from management. Healthy self-esteem gives and also receives what is fair. At the job interview you turn up in a position of power. They will be interviewing you but, in a way, you are interviewing them too.

Learn about the business and help them learn about you. Alignment will either be present, or it won't. If alignment between yourself and a person, place or job becomes obvious take this opportunity. Let the interviewer know how you match the requirements.

You have learned what the job entails and the employer has learnt about you, now go ahead and grasp the opportunity. For a fashion job, dress the part, compliment the interviewer's outfit and mention that you are creative. In the interview share 3-4 of your strengths that relate to the job specifically.

Say words to the effect, "I am great at colour matching. I like to make people feel confident through fashion. I love fashion design. I enjoy creative work on my own and in a small team. I get a good feeling about this place and am keen to learn more."

The interview is built up in our mind as a daunting challenge to overcome. The reason people are fearful is because they are trying to get a result of employment immediately, putting the cart before the horse.

Now when it does come time to sell yourself, isn't it great to know what the employer needs? You can address each point they made, by sharing how you will be of value. They can be truly impressed, as you **connect the dots** between job description and yourself. Steven will also hear that you have **been listening**, which is remarkable, since 80% of people don't do it well.

JOB ALIGNMENT

During the self-esteem chapter we chatted about how it is not arrogant to recognise your good qualities. Deflating oneself is low-self-esteem. This is where someone perceives themselves less valuable. Exaggerating oneself is high self-esteem. This is where someone perceives themselves more valuable, than reality.

Healthy self-esteem is the truth – an accurate self-image. You have great qualities. It is a reliable path to confidence, to believe what is true about yourself. You are important in a way that is honest. You can share your strengths at the interview and people will pick up on this authenticity.

- I understand that I have strengths and limitations
- I care about myself **and** the company
- All people are valuable including myself
- I can share my value with others
- I match my value with the desired job

Healthy self-esteem is recognised as confidence grounded in reality. I am who I am. I do not minimise nor exaggerate myself, instead share what is true.

Let's say you have been out of the job-hunting game for a long time. Where is it best to start? Work out what you want and need. Are there benefits you need this job to provide? It could be monetary reward, bonuses, great location, holiday pay, flexible hours, work/family balance, great leadership team, high morale, socialising, fulfilment doing work you like.

For example, if needing somewhere close to home, less pay might be acceptable. When working in a remote area you can expect a higher salary. If flexibility is needed to take care of family, then some work-from-home shifts can be negotiated up front.

Don't accept a role that throws your important needs out the window. You probably won't stick with it. Be honest in the interview. There is more chance for you and the employer to get a desired outcome. Make a list of what you need and weigh up how much wiggle room you are okay with.

Details you might look for in a job interview:

- The pay rate, bonuses and commission structure
- Opportunities for advancement and promotion
- Training, education and upskilling provided
- If the business is family friendly, offers insurance, flexible hours

- Option to work some shifts from home
- Whatever perks are important to you

There are certain traits an employer looks for. Interviewers aren't always wanting highly charismatic people. It's usually not even on their hiring criteria. They are however looking for effort. Does a person's attitude in a job interview reveal their work ethic? It sure does. You are not meant to perform perfectly. Instead, give your care and attention.

Employers are looking to hire someone eager to learn. Most things can be taught but someone unwilling isn't one of them. This fact takes the pressure away. Showing care and effort are achievable goals for anyone. Eagerness will make you memorable amongst your lazy counterparts. What the employer is looking for:

- Showing effort
- You are trustworthy (do what you say)
- Not under or over-qualified
- Following instructions
- If you are a match for the job

LOW JOB MOTIVATION

Deidre worked in a small department of a large organisation. She completed important work however found herself slacking off on lesser priority duties. Doing 'just the minimum' was well below her usual standard. Motivation was low and anxiety high.

A new position was advertised from within the company that interested Deidre. Maybe a change would spark her energy? She wanted the role but believed that a fellow employee, Barbara was a better match for the promotion. This belief had further lowered her motivation.

Deidre said, "Barbara is the favourite and I am a clear 2nd choice. If she gets promoted first, then I will be next in line. Why should I work hard when I have to wait so long for the reward? Procrastination has spilled over into my home life too. House cleanliness and healthy eating had fallen away."

Me: "I think the possibility of promotion going to someone else was hard to come to terms with. The focus on future promotion has taken you out of the present and then imagining no reward coming your way. It makes sense motivation has been low. Much of life-force is used up in anxious imaginations, playing in your mind."

Patience for reward is a wonderful discipline to master, at work and home.

Me: "At some level the low motivation will be felt by others around you. We want your colleagues seeing you energised which gives you the best chance of success. I think there is a way to switch your energy back on. This interview process is an opportunity to shine. Over the next few weeks put your best foot forward at work and home.

Each day bring your focus to the 'now.' Wear your best outfits and remember why you like this job in the first place. You love data entry and being organised. Let the reward be daily success, not a 'possible' future achievement. Keep the promotion back of mind and prioritise your work satisfaction in the present.

Instead of focusing on Barbara's work and a negative future, it is worth getting back in touch with your own performance. You are already good at the work and love it most of the time. Being at your best has no downsides. It gives you a chance of promotion this time and an almost certainty for the next opportunity."

Eating habits can affect mood and energy. To support Deidre physically I suggested cutting out the diet sodas and replacing with water. There was also meal skipping, so recommended a standard portion of real food for breakfast, lunch and dinner.

Me: "Fasting, with diet soft drinks is problematic. Metabolism and energy will be too scattered. Cravings for sugar will also be increased and escalate the issue you've been having with motivation.

Let's get you back to a consistent flow with work, and energy coming from quality food choices. Rather than future focus I suggest present moment care at work and home."

She realised that showing initiative would let them know she is serious about advancing in the company. I offered that she could engage in conversation with management prior to the interview, for information gathering (knowledge that leads to confidence). Information gives us the means to make better decisions.

During the conversation, if the role is aligned say something like this: "I'm excited for the opportunity to apply! Data entry is my speciality as you know and making sure your business is protected is important to me. I heard you mention a qualification I don't have yet. I'll complete that over the next 2 weeks and look forward to giving you everything I've got. I will keep stepping up for you as needed."

If the new job is not a match for you: "Thanks for all the information. That job might not be the ideal match but I think Barbara would fill that role very well. As you know I love and thrive with data entry and systems. Please do keep me in mind if advancement opens up in that area. I will keep stepping up for you as required!"

We set the goal to improve performance and find out if the job is a value match (aligned). This is achievable.

ENTITLEMENT SYNDROME

When I applied for work some years ago, I knew the operations manager. I didn't assume the job would just be given to me though, this would be presumptuous. I asked questions about what they were looking for. After listening I could truthfully say I was willing to take care of their customers and company.

History with a friend boosts confidence because familiarity and knowledge are present. Even so, I have no right to be hired automatically by a close friend or family. This is someone's livelihood and company I'm going into. I wanted to show commitment to the job and appreciation for being considered. It's his decision who to let on the team and thankfully I was accepted.

Affirmation: *"I care about myself and the employer's needs too."*

Entitlement syndrome is the belief that I should be chosen just because I turn up or know a guy. Commitment and effort aren't even needed. I can be casual (unprepared) and the employer will somehow look past a nonchalant attitude, mistaking it for confidence. They will pick me over people who cared and did their best. This attitude will not be effective.

Job Application Instructions

Another friend owns a virtual assistant service that caters to health professionals. Those who work for her don't need prior experience, as training is fully provided. On the job they are expected to follow procedures, such as filing documents correctly and ensuring confidential items are only sent to authorised people.

When advertising for new staff there are specific instructions for applicants to complete. Would-be-employees are to apply by email and answer 2 questions. They are asked not to send a resume at this time and wait for a reply from management. That's it. Should be easy, right?

Out of the last group of 60 applicants, only 12 correctly followed instructions. This begs the question: If the majority won't do as asked, then why would they follow procedure when hired? The remaining 48 people don't get a call-back. Those who read the job description and followed instructions are the only ones to get an interview.

She doesn't need a resume to be sent because personality and ability to listen are revealed right from the start. A simple request to care about the instructions was given and 80% of people didn't.

Some people phoned about the job and sent no email. Others replied to the ad but didn't answer the questions. A large number of people did anything but do what was asked. The percentage of those who don't listen (80%) has held firm over several years, she informed me.

If anxiety could speak it would say: "I'll do it my way, even to my own detriment."

It is a great result of healing, to perform correct action, ignoring Ego and anxiety.

AM I DOING WHAT I'M SUPPOSED TO BE?

As human beings we sometimes need to observe ourselves. The purpose of this is to make sure subconscious programming isn't blocking our path forward. Why do I act against self-interest? Is high anxiety getting in the way?

The habit of not listening can be born out of desire for self-protection. Doing it my way feels right, even though sometimes it is not. Rationally we know that following quality instructions give results but a fear of being vulnerable leads to sabotaging behaviours that push people and opportunities away.

The deeper reason behind this, is avoiding being seen as inadequate (not enough). And the fear alongside that is rejection. The higher anxiety is, the more often we self-sabotage. It is an subconscious protection behaviour, associated with the amygdala brain functions. When I self-sabotage no one can embarrass me. I use rejection first, denying anyone a chance to reject me!

Being conscious enough to be just outside your comfort zone is valuable. A combination of expressing your personality and taking right action is recommended.

It is worth understanding the nature of anxiety inside and out. With understanding we gain a greater ability to transform. Anxiety is not a proportional response to reality. In fact, a constant fear of life and missing our goals is worse than possibly feeling embarrassed. Make a point to base decisions on what will give the best results.

See if you can make choices in accordance with your highest thoughts. Therapy, gaining knowledge, personal reflection, weighing up options, strategies and self-acceptance all activate cerebrum brain functions. With this brain region active, more often, we feel in control. The sooner we use mindfulness the better.

Following instructions means we put aside Ego and do what is asked. By doing so two very cool things happen: 1) You get to learn about someone else's way of doing things. You can try out what they've offered and take from that, what works. 2) You are intelligently not sabotaging yourself now.

The opposite of sabotage is correction. Don't repeat your mistakes, correct them.

I don't need to be right, but it is useful to take correct action. Intelligently not self-sabotaging pre-supposes that taking a quality action is far better than trying to appear right or smart. The fear of looking stupid (and Ego) drops away and better results follow.

We can observe that correct action would come from the cerebrum, which is the rational part of our brain. Thoughts from the cerebrum might sound like this this. "This is the best course of action based on data. This makes sense for my body and mind. I am open to grow as a person by trying something new."

- I can do what is beneficial even if anxiety tries to sabotage me
- I can say 'yes' when circumstances are aligned
- I can gain knowledge to feel more comfortable
- I can complete what I have been putting off for years
- These are achievable for everyone

I will take action against self-sabotage, while incorporating safety, confidence and self-acceptance.

ASK A QUESTION, MAYBE GET HIRED

When I used to apply for jobs, my favourite trick was to visit the location and chat with the receptionist. I'd say, "Hi, I'm thinking about applying for a position. How do people normally get hired here?" I would also ask, "What needs does the *company* have at the moment?" and "What is it like to work here?"

I'd ask just 2-3 natural questions, respecting their valuable time but if chatty, plenty of useful information could be garnered. I thank the receptionist when leaving and note their name, so I can mention them at my interview.

Part way through the interview, you share: "I popped in and chatted to Janice, a few days ago, I hope that's okay. She was very helpful. I liked when she said everyone here gets along well and you really are customer focused. I'll work to uphold your standards. I believe I can contribute by doing accurate work and creating a happy customer who keeps coming back."

Will this make you memorable? Yes, you made an effort to care about their business. They will probably ask Janice about your interaction and she'll report you were friendly and thankful. Once again you are more likely to make a good impression because you took time to understand and care about the company's needs.

My record time for getting employed was 2 minutes. While asking the receptionist a question, the boss walked by and I got introduced. I inquired, "Hi, I'm looking for a change of career, what is required to be hired?" He told me what course to undertake and that I could start upon completion. I was inexperienced and no position was advertised.

It's a no resistance question. Asking, appreciates the fact that being hired isn't a given; there are steps and you are **willing** to take them. This means the manager doesn't have to commit but can tell you the **hiring pathway**. They could refer you to the place down the road or make you an offer. An introduction by their own trusted team member is just icing on the cake.

An example at the airport, "We want someone very safety focused. Regulations need to be followed strictly." You reply, "Great I'll complete a health and safety course online before attending the interview next week. I follow your airline and the travel industry online. I like helping people and look forward to giving my best."

Note: A statement like this works well when you are prepared to follow through and the job is genuinely aligned with who you are.

If you don't get the chance to chat to a receptionist, you can still ask a few questions at the interview. Personally, I would let the manager speak first and if they don't happen to reveal much about their needs, I would clarify what they are before talking about myself.

Asking the question, "What do you need?" makes you memorable and shows care.

By caring about the business being approached, you will immediately be in the top 20% of applicants. Probably even the top 5%. Confidence will be high for a reason. Being **prepared**, having insider **knowledge** and **sharing value** based on fulfilling their needs, should give you confidence.

LEANING IN SOCIALLY

I used to get very anxious at cafes and restaurants. In small groups there was nowhere to hide whereas large crowds were easy to blend into. I didn't like coffee or know how to order correctly either. I felt too visible and wanted to leave. Knowledge and alignment were missing. I was an outsider in a place filled with anxious triggers. I would refuse most offers to catch up with someone at a café. It was just too hard.

In my early adulthood the mission was to leave as soon as possible. Trying to survive a social event is like being prey, ready to be pounced upon by embarrassment and nervous energy. Think deer trying to escape lion. That's what it was like for me many, many times. Wanting to escape was a regular part of my social experience.

Moving ahead several years, my attitude in visiting cafes changed. I began networking with fellow therapists and business owners, which I enjoyed. There was a structure to follow and a purpose for being there. And presently enjoyment at cafes include buying someone a special birthday breakfast. I found when the purpose for going somewhere was strong (aligned), anxiety dropped away.

Make sure that visiting a person, place or situation makes sense to you. Give yourself permission to be authentic with your likes and dislikes. Sticking with the hunt or be hunted analogy, don't go just to survive. Go hunting for a great coffee and enjoyment! Go seek new information while job hunting! Go hunting for your favourite breakfast! Lean into the social opportunity.

They call it job hunting. Not job surviving.

I am usually introverted, enjoying home and nature to recharge. Occasionally though, I want to be outgoing and centre of attention. I find that 'leaning into' a social situation helps considerably. If I am going to be somewhere, I will 'be there fully.' At a café I'll ask whether to order from the counter or table? At a social gathering I'll introduce myself and compliment people.

An initial instinct when socialising is to hold back and avoid people. Being in the background protects but it might feel as though you are prey to social embarrassment. A social situation is an opportunity to feel excitement, connection, happiness, have fun and create memories.

I honour my usual nature of introversion but when socialising, I will lean into the atmosphere. If I am going out it is worth making the most of it. You can be proud of yourself for socialising with anxiousness. You felt it and decided to carry on forward. **Courage** is feeling vulnerability and going for it anyway.

'Leaning in' means we might feel some nervousness but cross over, from avoidance, to action. Like Laura we met in the Power of Intention chapter, who previously had high social anxiety. She was triggered by many social scenarios, including going to the park with her daughter. She mentally prepared for the day to go well and fully leant into it. Both mum and daughter had a brilliant time.

Taking her daughter to the park is aligned with Laura's values of fitness, family and fun, so being overwhelmed doesn't belong there. Leaning in accepts that anxiety is possible. With that done, and out of the way, focus can be placed fully on enjoyment. When aligned, be present with the place and people you find yourself with.

It is brave to have been through adversity and chose a healing path. There might be some difficult days but you are progressing. All progress is worthy. You can be very proud of yourself head to toe, up, down, left, right, body, mind and spirit that you did it!

Set your main aim for steady progress. Avoid an all or nothing approach when socialising. 'All' would represent trying to achieve flawless, extraordinary and perfect social charm. 'Nothing' would represent everything as a disaster, I am not enough and everybody is judging me. Both extreme positive and negative perspectives are not stable, yet steady progress based on healing is.

If worried about what other people think, I suggest training yourself out of this habit. Personally, I think about what is most important to me. What does my heart want? I will focus on the answer and take 1-2 actions every day to get closer to my goal. The answer to, "What does my heart want?" is more important than judgment from others.

Along your path of healing, acknowledge your progress. Affirm before, during and after. "I'm doing it. Good for me. This is an achievement. I am safe. I am okay. This person, place or job is right for me."

SOCIAL REJECTION FREEDOM

Earlier we explored together the Alternative Meaning Technique. This is used to find several new perspectives that can heal disempowering beliefs, like I am not enough. In social situations, rejection hurts. It hurts more when the mind exaggerates objective reality. That is, anxiety attaching false or negative meanings to an event.

When rejected, anxiety might conclude that I did something wrong or am not enough. There are plenty of 'unhelpful meanings' our mind makes up. The path away from anxious beliefs is the Alternative Meaning Technique. We can observe our beliefs and re-install new ones.

My client mentioned she was making plans to catch up with a friend but had heard nothing for 2 days. She started to assign meanings about the lack of contact. The friend could be rude, got distracted or some other reason entirely. They could have a damaged phone so can't text back. It is possible she is buying a gift right now. We simply didn't know.

More information was needed before making any solid conclusions. Certainty evaporates anxiety and can lead to higher understanding. I mentioned how there is no meaning YET because knowledge is missing. There could be an acceptable or unacceptable explanation.

A caring message was sent to the friend and it turned out she was going through a difficult situation, where safety was at risk. Those anxious thoughts were replaced with compassion. Space was needed to process the ordeal she had been through.

Understanding was only possible because she sought to gain more knowledge about her friend. Rather than focusing on the no reply, care could be shown. Later they enquired about how their friend is holding up, which opened communication from the heart. Anxiety about no communication, turned into care.

We simply do not have the evidence to assume what people think about us and that rejection is bad. With communication lines open, anxiety is closed down. What can anxiety say when up against truth, understanding, compassion and love? Not much.

An anxiety disorder is the ingrained, chronic habit of believing imagination over objective reality. Anxiety makes up stories without evidence necessary to do so. The truth sets us free from a negative imagination. While I am seeking truth and thinking realistically, anxiety is closed down.

If my mind is giving me beliefs based on truth and experience, I will reflect on these thoughts. I will not dwell on exaggerated falsehood, nor wild accusations and imagined problems that don't exist. When anxiety calls, hang up the phone. Say, "I'm not accepting your calls anymore. I will find out what actually is true."

If you find that anxiety is making up stories, use your inner dialogue to heal those thoughts. Affirm: "This situation has no concrete meaning. I assign meaning based on the facts. I can't know the whole truth but I can get very close by seeking knowledge. Furthermore, my self-esteem and self-worth are intact and not defined by rejection. I accept myself and others as they are."

The point here is to make conclusions based on evidence. Once you have gathered information and taken the time to think things through to the closest point of truth, you won't be believing the nonsense from anxiety.

Place a high value on what is known and anxiety will evaporate.

Here are more than a dozen other possibilities for rejection or not connecting with someone in a social setting:

1. They are stressed from work
2. They just experienced an intense situation
3. They are not a personality match
4. They are a lousy listener
5. They are abrupt or dismissive
6. They are distracted, not present
7. They are not interested in the particular topic being discussed
8. The topic being discussed triggers their anxiety, so they retreat
9. The environment is too loud for them
10. The environment is not to their liking for another reason
11. I am too hungry or thirsty
12. Not eating makes me ungrounded
13. I am the distracted one, not present
14. Not all connection is instant and perfect
15. Rejection serves a purpose. It allows me to re-prioritise

16. I am nervous near this person because they are actually not for me
17. I am so excited to be free of this person
18. There is no specific meaning. There is nothing to fix

Anxiety makes it uncomfortable when a social interaction doesn't go well. The truth is we don't know what state another human being is in. They could very well be going through grief, stress, overwhelm and sparing us their drama. Without knowledge of what is truly going on, there is no reason to draw negative conclusions.

I am not going to drive myself into anxiety by guessing what people are thinking. Try this strategy instead, next time you are guessing someone else's mind. Walk up to them. Say here is what I am thinking and feeling. What are you thinking and feeling? Compare notes and form a conclusion.

This list is a wonderful reminder that there is nothing wrong with us. We are not going to connect with every person perfectly at the first meeting.

AS-ISSING

A speaker I worked with in 2013 was due to give the most important speech of her career. Nichole looked out towards the audience. She was well prepared and confident, illuminated by the stage light above. Ready and wearing high heels, she walked on stage, tripped over and fell flat on her face.

Although mishaps and challenges are painful, there is an opportunity to turn the tables in our favour. An apparent social disaster can even be advantageous, by using as-issing. This is a mental strategy of using what happens as a resource. As-issing is an intention that can be carried inside. Whatever happens I will not judge but use it to my advantage.

"I get knocked down but I get up again. You are never going to keep me down."
Song by Chumbawamba

Nichole got up, dusted herself off, re-attached her smile after the shock and said, "Clearly, I have just fallen down! But that's what can happen in life. Sometimes you fall down. It's what you do after that counts. You can stay down, get angry, run away, bury your head in the sand or simply carry on."

She then started her presentation. There were no thoughts of doom or catastrophe, just because gravity caused her physical body to meet the floor. Nichole has done the work, preparing her mind for challenges. Her intention for years has been "carry on" and that is what she did.

Challenges can be viewed as detrimental or not. Embodying a mantra of "carry on" and falling to the ground, presents a perfect opportunity to demonstrate, said mantra. The topic of her speech gets a real-life metaphor to boot. These types of mishaps are usually part of completing a larger vision.

People, circumstances and your environment are all possible resources.

Interruptions can make the end result even better. After falling to the floor, she had the audience's complete attention and used the story to discuss resilience. What better way to share her message than to demonstrate. Kramer the TV character on 'Seinfeld' fell over when first entering the room. This was not scripted but became his trademark entrance over several seasons.

It is true Nichole fell down but objectively it doesn't mean anything. She used the situation as a teaching moment because she could. There was a strong purpose inside her to help people so embarrassment was not there. My offering to you, is that you can empower your mind to respond the way you want it to. We need as-issing – an attitude of carrying on, to fulfil our mission.

As-issing can be used to break tension with your audience. It is often trust-building to share vulnerability in a social situation. This is true on stage, in relationships and at interviews. There is very little resistance when we are working with reality. You use what you've got, in the present moment. This means 'leaning into' your current situation.

Can I acknowledge my reality and even look for an advantage? Can I carry on when anxiety is telling me it's a terrible disaster? Sure, give it a try!

THE PURSUIT OF HEALING

In the book and movie 'The Pursuit of Happiness,' Chris Gardner earns a life-changing job opportunity. Being hired at this company means the difference between providing for his son or ongoing poverty. Shortly before the interview, he is arrested for unpaid parking tickets. After sorting out paperwork at the police station he has only minutes to make it on time.

Chris knows he is woefully underdressed (still wearing his painting outfit). With no time to change out of scruffy clothes, he gives it his best shot. He answers all the questions adequately in front of the managers dressed in suits but his appearance can't be ignored. After some discussion the boss asks, "What would you say if a guy walks into an interview without a shirt on and I hired him?"

Chris Gardner replies with continuing confidence, "He must have had on some really nice pants!"

There is a nice dialogue in the interview, where the boss asks if he wants to learn this business and has **already started** researching on his own? Chris replies, "Yes sir." The fact Chris already started probably made a big difference in the end. The value of initiative to acquire knowledge cannot be overestimated.

Chris was not dressed well but carried on and took the opportunity to show people he would not be held back by adversity. His effort and fight for the job shone through. The interviewer chuckled and appreciated that he didn't give up. He showed a fighting spirit, which is a credit to his potential role as a salesman at the company.

As-issing is the power of utilisation. You use whatever occurs to your advantage or to build rapport. You carry on. As-issing is a genuine statement about what is occurring. It is not hiding from life. It is flipping a situation to work for us. Anxiety makes us believe that setbacks are catastrophes, causing us to retreat from wonderful experiences in life. These thoughts are no longer the boss of us.

If you have a business meeting where your outfit is ruined or stained. Say, "Clearly, I have just had a run in with the coffee machine. And it won. I mean no disrespect by how I am dressed. Please let this very rare incident, reflect that you are important to me (pause for a moment). I chose promptness over changing my clothes which would have made me late, impacting your day. Please receive this presentation with that in mind. I respect how important your time is."

You acknowledge what happened. You own it out loud. You keep focus on the mission.

Give yourself a great chance for social confidence and enjoyment:

- Practise your new tools for confidence
- Listen to increase familiarity and knowledge
- Take notes
- Clarify anything you don't understand
- Rehearse the event being excellent in your mind
- Check the person, place or thing is aligned with your goals
- Have a written list of your best character traits and the value you provide others
- Prior to an event, practise relaxed breathing and eat moderately
- Focus on the present moment, particularly as opposed to worrying about the future or dwelling on the past. Affirm: "In the present, I will gain knowledge then share my value. I am well prepared. They are lucky to have me"

'YEAH BUT' MONOLOGUE

Me: My body size is too skinny, yeah but my eyes are nice. I get anxious sometimes, yeah but I'm better than I used to be. Some parts of my body are hairy, yeah but that's okay. I get anxious sometimes, yeah but in certain environments I am very comfortable with myself. I get anxious sometimes, yeah but I love myself, strengths and with room for growth. I am not good enough, yeah but I have performed well hundreds of times in my life, probably several thousand times. Okay my eyebrows aren't masculine enough, yeah but my thighs are. Sometimes I let people down, yeah however I do my best and help many. But there really is something wrong with me mentally and I'm weak too, yeah that hurts a bit but there are 1000 things right with me. Mentally and physically, I've responded weakly at times. Other times with tremendous strength. I'm still here, aren't I? I have moved house on my own, carrying items down a steep driveway. I have run a half marathon when my back was seized 12 hours prior to the event. I played soccer with a broken foot. I have loved in relationships when all seemed lost. I scramble climbed a mountain at 3am in the pitch black with nothing but a small head torch. I have hiked in Africa amongst the wild beasts. I have been 12 feet from a wild rhino and swam with sharks. I have endured pain physically. Anxiety, you've got it wrong I am strong and sturdy. I am wild and worthy. To pretend that I am weak is laughable at this stage, honestly. I love myself and by the way, anxious thoughts, I love you too... I'm seeing you as an opportunity now. You were covering over parts of myself I was embarrassed about and didn't want others to see. I'm done hiding because that reinforces it's not okay to be who I am. The reality of me is far greater than any made up fake version. Best of all, it is real. I am dealing with reality. Now I can keep some parts tucked away to share with a few and other parts will share with many. Both are okay. There's no rules here. If I choose to share more parts of myself, well, there's just more to love.

You, Anxiety are the part that tries to protect me from myself and others but in doing so making them wrong. I can be conservative if I want to. I can express myself to the whole world if I want to. I'm not meant to be full of myself thinking I'm perfect or anything like that but I will own the truth of my magnificence. I am, and all people are magnificent and worthy of self-acceptance and love. It's through conflict and challenges that the world changes. It's through conflict and challenges that I evolve. There was never anything wrong with me just an unrealistic expectation to perform a certain way. Perform for who? And why? Who knows! I'm not your puppet, anxiety. Anxiety you are a squeaky wheel on a bike, not the captain of my life and when I grease you up with enough self-love, self-awareness, truth and safety to satiate you. I have healed in the present moment.

Anxiety is a little quieter now.

You're hopeless, yeah but I'm not because I'm still trying. This is my breakthrough. I am safe. I am loveable. I am unstoppable in my healing. Every day I take forward action even if a little anxious voice tries to slow me down. Something bad will happen, yeah but if I do nothing positive, negative stuff happens anyway. I might as well go for my best life. Going for it makes me feel alive. Treading over ground I have never crossed before, being astonished at what life provides when I follow my heart. Yes, I sure am okay that it doesn't turn out perfect. Yes, I sure am okay that people will support and challenge me. I expect good and bad to happen equally on this journey I have chosen to undertake. Carry on, I will.

You're going to fail, yeah but I'm not. If I put myself out there to win, each time I'll get better, I'll learn more, I'll ask for help because I'm not doing it alone this time. I'm in this for the long term and I know I won't be perfect. I will work my way towards excellence. Knowledge is extremely abundant and accessible at this time in history. Michael Jordan missed the cut from his college team for not being good enough, according to some coach. Why would we listen to people's limiting opinions or anxiety's imaginations? I keep my focus on the target. Be present. Be present. Be present. My job is to accept and love myself.

HEALING FOOD ANXIETY

All human behaviour attempts to fulfil a need. We will look closely at our emotional fulfilment and how food works vs doesn't work to meet these needs. Does excessive eating occur when anxious, tired and looking for comfort? Reflect if you have a tendency toward emotional eating.

A large number of the world's population unfortunately struggle with their food choices. At different stages in life binging on food and at other times trying to rebalance with a restrictive diet. It is stressful to the digestive and nervous systems when food habits are out of balance.

While food can be enjoyable, it is not a healing method for emotions such as anxiety. Emotions are related to our thoughts, beliefs, nervous system and life experiences. A chocolate bar has never improved my perspective about life nor improved self-esteem.

Addictive food is so ineffective at healing emotions, as evidenced by cravings to fill the same void again next time. We get addicted to emotional eating because it doesn't work. Why after eating so much sugar did I continue to crave? Because I was seeking to feel better via a source that cannot provide.

You deserve a better way to satisfy your deeper needs such as healing, self-nurturing, love and healthy self-esteem.

A healthy relationship with food can be balanced and satisfying. Balance means equilibrated, moderate, the middle ground. To be lacking is not satisfying and neither is over-consumption. The desired result is fulfilling physical hunger, which is moderate (satisfying).

Balanced habits are possible. After eating you will feel light and well afterwards. Beware of any extreme food recommendations you hear from others on your journey toward health. If it doesn't look after you physically, mentally and emotionally steer clear.

You might like to mindfully ask these questions each day:

- What result am I wanting to achieve with food?
- Are current habits making me feel well?
- Is my digestion giving feedback?
- Do my food choices look after physical health?
- What does a great relationship with food look like to me?

BEAT THE TREATS

There are motivational reasons (or drivers) for food compulsions. "It's just a treat, it won't hurt. I don't want to be the odd one missing out, when everyone eats whatever they want. I need sweets after a meal. This is my comfort food. It's a reward."

But why do we make unhealthy choices? Anxiety. Because anxiety is telling us that a 'bad' thing is a 'good' thing.

A modern lifestyle is filled with so many convenient treats. We are in pleasure overload but feeling worse than ever. The body is over-stimulated then compensates by giving us symptoms like anxiety, fatigue and illness to break our urge for indulgence.

If I ate big chocolate desserts every day for 1 month there will be little to no genuine satisfaction at the end of it. The pleasure will be over mere seconds afterwards. The massive surge of 'quick energy' from processed foods, is a shock to the body. Perhaps after such a surge of stimulation, the body slams the brakes to slow us down. It makes sense why there is a term called 'sugar crash.'

The concept of having a treat every day is paradoxical. By definition a treat is, "an event or item that is out of the ordinary and gives great pleasure." To make things a treat again, have them rarely. Also, explore rewards and comforts for the body, that are not food related at all. See if you can satisfy your need with a healing alternative.

Satisfy your need, not the craving.

Rather than guilty pleasures, I much prefer pleasure that is satisfying, without the guilt and shame. It is addictive behaviour to chase constant pleasure, ignoring downsides. A treat that makes us feel awful isn't really a treat anymore, is it?

Although addictions are used to avoid pain, they also cause pain in equal measure. Comfort eating leads to feeling uncomfortable in our body. Too many sweets for reward seems like a punishment. Too much wine makes us feel less than fine. Bread can make me feel like lead and takeaway can take away my energy.

The distinction to make is, being purposeful. You can eat food for a purpose. Savor cuisine that makes you feel light, well and energetic afterward. If it's easy to digest and comes from the Earth, it is probably going to satisfy you. Include textures, spices and flavours that appeal to you.

To be satisfied, means you feel fulfilled during and after the meal. We place attention on all the tasty, healthy-type foods and incorporate more of them into your weekly lifestyle. Healing doesn't mean no enjoyment. It means truly satisfying the body and living a great life, according to your values.

Emotion-based eating is the problem to overcome if you want mastery of food habits and weight control.

ADAM'S STORY

I have worked with a number of clients who eat just once per day. Many were considered heavier than medically healthy. A gentleman named Adam believed that since he was already 110kg, he had better restrict to one meal per day. He thought that since he was consuming just a single meal, it needed to be worth it. "I better make sure it's a big one."

This is an example of both under-eating and over-eating. A minimal number of meals but over-consuming at the lunch event. Adam either had a big plate of fried chicken or multiple sandwiches packed with meat and salad. This meal over-filled him. He intended for less calories overall, leading to weight loss but it wasn't working.

Note: Meal plans are not moral issues. Ultimately there are no good or bad foods, just consequences. There are food tendencies that increase anxiety and weight problems, and you are capable of correcting what is not working.

Determine if something is working. Are food choices balanced? Is the current plan realistic? Would a dietician consider it functional? When we checked if Adam's habits were aligned with his wellness goal, the answer was "not aligned." If the food is too heavy and the amount is substantial, our digestion will be stressed.

The intention Adam had was that he didn't want to be hungry. His only sitting had to last 24 hours, when he would again overfill himself. The solution for Adam and the rest of us, is to spread the satisfaction over 3-5 meals. Regular sized portions of real food are easy to digest and therefore moderate.

Along the journey you will meet people who suggest extreme food lifestyles. They will state that it 'works for them' and 'you should try it too.' A throw away recommendation from a celebrity, friend or family member will not take into account all of your needs and the implications of 'risky weight loss tricks.' Some of which will negatively impact metabolism, digestion and mood for years to come.

A Health Practitioner will probably recommend a lifestyle that sounds boring but it is designed to make you feel truly healthy. I am only interested in systems designed to heal body and mind. Following far-fetched fads and medication trends could set you back years in your relationship with food.

I have heard of the cake diet, the no water diet, the meat diet and the potato diet. Please make it stop! A quick technique used to trick the body into weight loss is risky. I'm not willing to take on health risks myself or for clients. In a consultation with me, we work on healing from the start, which looks like the following.

- Meals that promote digestive ease
- Food variety, textures, seasoning, quality and enjoyment
- Eating to satisfy physical hunger
- Clearing sugar cravings
- Healing emotional eating
- Reduction in reflux, bloating and other symptoms
- Reduction in heaviness
- Boosting metabolism
- Increasing energy
- Better sleep
- Plenty of water

I will not recommend:

- Amphetamines for weight loss
- Meat only diets
- Raw vegetable only diets
- Chocolate diets
- Restrictive or temporary food plans
- Dangerous fads that do not care for the whole body

A relationship with food can be functional, relaxed and satisfying. If a food plan is making you feel obsessed or emotional, let's work on a better plan together.

FOOD AND SUCCESS ANXIETY

Sarah had reached a high-level position in an organisation. She was the only female executive amongst a dozen male colleagues and valued a professional image and work ethic at all times.

Sarah came to see me because she could successfully lose weight but gains it all back within 3 months. She said, "I can eat flawlessly for several weeks, no carbs, bread or alcohol. People comment how I've lost weight and look amazing, but the praise makes me so anxious. I just want to escape!"

Sarah: "I cringe at positive comments and kind of freak out. I gain all the weight back as quick as physically possible. I want to be invisible... or more accurately, not noticed for my body. When I am a medium build, work gets noticed but when slim, my body gets focused on. There is a pattern of self-sabotage. I can flawlessly eat but after getting praised, it all goes out the window."

On multiple occasions she has lost weight and regained it. 2 things that caught my attention were 'flawless eating' and the 'freak out' upon becoming slim.

FLAWLESS EATING

By what measure do we label something flawless? Had she reached a point of perfection? Is eating excellent but still with a lingering fear of failure? Sarah used a strict Keto diet, able to cut out all carbs, no worries.

Me: "It is an achievement to eat healthy however consider if this is satisfying long-term. Under ideal conditions you have cut out carbs and lost weight however life presents us with tricky situations periodically such as: birthdays, seasonal holidays, work celebrations, stressful days and travel. When these occur, moderation is useful."

Continued: "Because ideal conditions are impermanent, habits vary dependent on the occasion. This cycle of being flawless and loose is quite dramatic, creating up and down weight change over the course of a year. You have been oscillating between sacrifice and indulgence, which are big swings in food consumption."

An idea I present to clients is to make your good and bad days similar, moderated. Think of the tallest building you can. A towering skyscraper with a large crane on top. Hanging off this crane is a long rope and pendulum. When this pendulum is pulled out horizontally and then dropped, it will swing back and forth via the force of gravity.

In a pendulum diet the person swings from one side to another, rarely settled in the middle. On one side is restricted eating and on the other side is indulgence. When you stop swinging between the extremes you will start to feel steady. Think balanced, not perfect.

Sarah was considering the analogy. Being perfect with food had never held up long term and in all conditions. It seemed really clear to her now. Every few months she sabotaged, feeling frustrated. Is there a middle ground between 'flawless eating' and 'indulgent eating?'

FREAK OUT

The other factor, freaking out about being slim would be even more relevant. The 'freak out' suggested there was at least one fear about being slim. When Sarah's body gets noticed at work, it makes her cringe. Where weight loss feels comfortable for some, it triggered anxiety for Sarah.

Sarah's self-worth was linked to career. In her perception, being slim is a disadvantage to professional image and career progression. "I have persevered at the firm and want my work to speak for itself. I want my results to shine rather than me."

She has made an assessment. There is something risky about being slim. Was it about being focused on too much for sex appeal? Getting noticed less for stellar work performance? Not wanting the suspicion of special treatment because of physical appearance?

A smaller or larger body might have no effect on getting promoted. Unknowns that we believe to be true are anxiety. The best solution may be to keep focus on business. If she continues delivering millions of dollars' worth of revenue to the firm, chances are they will reward her primarily based on the value she brings.

Worry about career progression due to her figure is anxiety. Looks could be 5% or less than 0.1% of what makes her valuable to the company. No one can know for sure. Sarah has an inner conflict. A desire to be slimmer AND a desire for respect as an executive. Could she have both?

FITTING IN TO THE MAX

Jill, 48 years old told me that she drank 4 Pepsi Max cans every day. This had gone on for years. Her Mum and sister consumed other Pepsi varieties. Although sugarless drinks contain no calories, this fact does not exclude us from the side effects of increasing food cravings, slowing down fat burning, increased risk for type 2 diabetes and stroke. One thing is sure, sodas are not adding a health value.

"I'm boring and won't be accepted for who I am."

I assisted Jill to complete the Walker Addiction Removal Process. In the WARP, we uncover all the reasons for a compulsive behaviour. Every habit is made up of perceived advantages to the user. Some reasons are simple, like "I enjoy it." Others can be psychologically complex, like "avoiding emotions" and "fitting in with a group."

Jill revealed one the reasons she drank soft drink was to not be boring. I asked, "What does it mean to you if you are boring?"

She replied: "If I'm healthy all the time I won't be interesting enough and my family won't talk to me anymore. Giving up Pepsi makes me abnormal. They'll judge me for being too health focused and I'll get rejected. They will all leave me!"

There was anxiety behind the habit. Not enough or different, means rejection for being the odd one out. Earlier in life her brain made a connection between soft drinks and fitting in.

As a family they watch TV together, often insulting fit people and laughing at health trends. "Look at them working so hard, we're living the good life."

Humour covers over the tragedy of group illness. Their banter reinforces collective belief that 'health is abnormal.' Jill could see her mum and sister approaching 90-100kg but could not imagine herself turning up later in the year fit, energetic and drinking 2L-3L of water every day instead.

BREAKING THE NEWS

When it is time to let people know you have changed food and drink habits, keep it simple. There may be a period of adjustment for each member in the group. Be truthful so everyone knows what is going on. Remember knowledge and truth are 2 long-term healing solutions, allowing us to work with reality.

When offered soft drink you could say plainly what is true for you. Whether it's: "Thanks for the offer, I'm not thirsty." "Thanks for the offer, soft drinks aren't aligned with my body" Or "The soft drinks hurt my stomach. Thanks for thinking of me. I've got a water already."

The urge to fit in with family is strong and important. I assured Jill that what you choose to drink is a very small part of who you are. What makes you special to your mum and sister will always be there.

In the Walker Addiction Removal Process, we find ways to have every need accounted for. It's one thing to find the *reason for addiction* and another to fully *clear the emotional attachments* holding the habit in place. So, how do we make sure Jill feels secure that her family won't leave her?

Me: "Let's examine some of the ways you already connect with family. We'll explore what is true. What are the ways that assure you of fitting in?"

Jill: "Fun, games and time together."

Me: "Okay great so you all spend time together and have fun. What about knowing their personalities and life history? Is it something special to know these people for nearly 50 years and everything you have been through?"

Jill: "For me it's just talking and sharing about our day. We meet up once a week and text every day too."

Me: "What else?"

She answered: "Giving support and feeling supported."

Me: "The support you feel, is that meaningful to you? And the way you support back, is that meaningful to them?"

She nodded and I continued: "Ever any affection between you recently or in the past?"

Jill: "Both, we hug most times meeting up and always a big squeeze when we say goodbye."

Her heart opened. There was a recognition of the way they connect as a family. Little moments as well as deep and meaningful experiences over a long time period. There were thousands of hours, memories and heartfelt moments.

Me: "Are all of those ways you connect, more or less than what Pepsi Max provides in terms of family togetherness?"

Jill: "Definitely more. Pepsi Max is basically nothing. It is sometimes there, like we have some but it is just a small part, compared to everything we all share."

My suggestion for the next 2 weeks, was that Jill become present to the connection that exists with family. I offered that she could be mindful of love regularly. Feel the compliments in her heart. Be present when greeting them with a hug. Breathe in when the heart is joyful. Notice the smiles on their faces when you are in each other's company.

A mind balancing exercise can be useful to break food and drink compulsions. To find true perspective. This is what the WARP Walker Addiction Removal Process is for. You find out why you do it and how to get what you truly want.

The fear is, "I will be a boring healthy person, which means my family will abandon me." The truth is there are many, many ways she fits in and is interesting, that are above and beyond simply consuming soft drinks. This is an example of challenging an anxious belief with a healing perspective.

After Jill and I discussed family connection we went deeper on the themes of 'interesting' and 'boring' decisions:

Downsides of interesting drink choices for Jill:

- reflux
- mentally foggy
- tired afterwards
- addictive
- lesser sleep quality
- weight gain
- more doctor visits
- risk of diabetes type 2

Benefits of boring drink choices for Jill:

- healthy
- reliable
- looking after digestive health
- safe
- improve metabolism
- stable energy levels
- inspire others
- proud of self

The approach going forward would be 3-fold:

1. Simply notice any cravings or anxious feelings that arise.
2. Focus the mind and heart on love and thankfulness for family.
3. Awareness of the upsides and downsides of soft drinks and making the best choice for herself, in the present moment. The new choice would not be based on fear of rejection. Decisions

will include what is best for her body, not what anxiety says based on a false reality.

DAIRY RESTRICTION

Priya had a goal for healthy food eating. Over the last few years, dairy products resulted in her feeling sick and vomiting. I asked about the circumstances of how this happens. She could abstain from dairy easily but "always craved" it when visiting family and at times of celebration.

Me: "Have you had any insights about why you consume dairy?"

Priya: "I see everyone else having cheese and feel like I'm missing out. Even though it makes me sick I can't stop craving it."

She continued: "I don't want to be the fussy person with an allergy, who bothers people. I don't want to buy special dairy-free products or have family get different food just for me. It never used to make me sick. Why does it do this? Sometimes I eat it again to check if I'm still intolerant."

Me: "Your body has been giving you feedback about dairy. We don't say that it is good/bad, right/wrong. We just check, is this working for me in the present moment? I would encourage aligning with the reality you find for yourself. I don't believe you have an addiction. It is likely an anxiety problem."

She waited a moment to hear my evidence on this assessment.

Me: "Your brain has no urge for several days and even weeks at a time. When by yourself and with your partner, control isn't even needed. What is the dairy urge then? It only surfaces in social situations around your family. It is normal to desire being **part of the group** however it is anxiety to believe dairy is essential to fitting in."

Me: "Do you feel like it's easier socially to just say yes to dairy rather than make a fuss?"

Priya: "Yes, that's it."

Me: "Any anxious beliefs? These could include: I don't want to cause a problem. I don't want everyone to think I'm weird. I don't want to get un-invited from future social gatherings."

She partly raised her hand as I mentioned this list. "The right people will care about us and accommodate needs. If someone has a problem with you looking after your body, that is what we call an uncaring attitude on their part."

Me: "Caring for your body is a reasonable behaviour. It is considering your present moment situation and food needs. It is healthy self-esteem to care for your body."

The 2 known components of Priya's dairy craving are anxiety.

- Believing that dairy is needed to feel included and might be rejected if people find out about her food intolerance.
- Not wanting to burden others with her food needs. Believing oneself not enough or wrong to request an alternative.

Me: "High self-esteem makes demands that our needs are met. Low self-esteem sacrifices our needs and satisfies others first. Healthy self-esteem is different. Healthy behaviours are caring for self and others. In the case of finding an alternative to dairy (which makes you sick), having a lactose-free milk and cheese is a completely reasonable option."

FEELING BETTER

The path away from compulsions is to choose habits that make you feel good mentally, emotionally and physically. Healing is providing the body what it truly needs. The healthy option will not give you a high or change your circumstances overnight but it is moving in the direction of betterment.

Don't get so trapped on short term emotional comforts that you forget to look after your body.

The goal of getting treatment is to find a better way. I help people find a better way. Here are the possibilities that healing offers:

- Finding an alternative to the addiction that is so satisfying you don't ever relapse
- Practicing how to make friends with your subconscious mind and take control of your thinking
- A significant reduction in cravings
- A return to clarity, leading to balanced thoughts and eating habits
- A higher level of physical well-being
- Addressing any life issues that are incomplete
- Letting go of judgement and self-criticism
- Becoming present rather than caught up in anxious imagination

SLEEPING WELL

Elaine, 64 years old visited the clinic with an acute sleep problem. For 3 weeks she experienced insomnia, averaging only 2 hours deep rest per night. Elaine was getting 1/3 of the minimum sleep required for proper brain and body function.

What is healthy sleep? 1 hour and 30 minutes completes a sleep cycle. Getting 5 of these per night is ideal for a middle-aged adult, equating to 7.5 hours of rest. Getting 4 sleep cycles, is 6 hours of rest and the minimum required to avoid physical and mental impairment. This is an accurate sleep guide for most although each person has their individual needs.

Partially waking after a sleep cycle is normal. You roll over, have a sip of water and drift back off. Poor quality is when there is difficulty getting to sleep, staying asleep and waking exhausted, due to restlessness.

Back to Elaine. Although insomnia had only been there for 3 weeks, she was 100 hours behind over that time period. Missing that much sleep meant Elaine was fearful. It was serious and affecting all areas of her life. Health, family and her mind were all strained. She tried sleep hygiene tactics but her nervous system was overwhelmed. The fact that she sought help quickly is a credit to her.

Elaine had a difficult medical history. In her late fifties she underwent a hysterectomy and also had Hodgkin's Lymphoma (a cancer of the lymphatic system), which was treated via chemotherapy. She had adverse reactions to many types of medication since treatment, so she needed natural solutions when possible.

Note: I recommend every person uses natural solutions to support body and mind. Healing can correct imbalances with emotional turmoil and body chemistry.

I enquired about prior times when sleep was challenging. On 3 occasions Elaine had gone several weeks with insomnia. All the episodes occurred after feelings of not being safe.

1) Her medical challenges. 2) A child passing away and 3) Being trapped in a locked car. These all deeply distressed her and within days insomnia set in.

I listened to all the information and then asked about her lifestyle. It was encouraging that she had several healthy habits. She eats well, does yoga, meditates, dances and has a support network. With these good things already in place, I determined that missing a feeling of 'safety' was likely contributing to insomnia. (Elaine confirmed this, adding she dreads the evening period before bed).

3 things in Elaine's favour:

1. She had successfully treated acute insomnia before.
2. A lifestyle that included good self-care.
3. The cause of her insomnia was clear; feeling unsafe and a 'closed in' feeling.

She requested that I remedy with hypnotherapy, as this method had worked very well in the past. A doctor treated with hypnotherapy on each of her previous episodes however he was no longer available. Her sleep problem was caused by a type of post-traumatic stress. She was safe to go to sleep but didn't *feel* safe.

Hypnosis has a unique ability to change physiology. In Elaine's case we identified the problem and focused almost entirely on safety.

She knew consciously she was okay to sleep but the deeper part of her mind was still reacting from traumatic experiences. She felt helpless, without options, like she would never sleep again. This fear overwhelmed her.

> *Difficult life events created a post-traumatic response for Elaine. We created a plan where she would trust that natural sleep would return and be conscious of her present safe environment. With hypnotherapy, the calming parasympathetic nervous system activated. Within several days she was back sleeping long and deeply.*

OVERTIRED

What does over-tired mean? This occurs when a person is awake longer than their body can handle. The stress hormone cortisol (aids our ability to respond to life) becomes more present in the body which makes it harder to sleep. When overtired, it is more challenging to get quality rest.

Contrary to instinct, being exhausted doesn't help create balanced sleep patterns. Over-tiredness can hinder quality sleep, just as it does with babies and toddlers. An overwhelmed child may be unable to rest due to cortisol, resulting in tantrums and wailing. Many parents can relate to this.

Cortisol in our bloodstream allows us to tackle challenges and take action (Elaine would have had higher than normal cortisol levels due to high stress). **We don't want our nervous system hyped up before bedtime.** The body is ready for action even though you are meant to be slowing down.

- Tired: The sleepy signal, resulting in melatonin release for deep rest.
- Overtired: A stress response, resulting in cortisol release for taking action.

Normal tiredness, in conjunction with time of day prompts the release of melatonin. It is possible to be present to the early signs of tiredness and prepare for sleep at this time each evening.

We want to release general stress prior to becoming exhaustion. This will gradually lower active cortisol levels leading to easier and deeper sleep. Being calm just before bed is useful but also at regular intervals. If you tend to be busy all day without breaks, your nervous system could be in need of calming rest.

DARREN'S STORY

Darren, 45 years old resided in Brisbane. He held a position with the Australian Defence Force and had previously deployed overseas, in combat situations. Darren would drive the vehicles on tour because of is his unique ability to remain alert, with little effort, for 24-36 hours.

Upon leaving the military he said sleep quality was relatively okay. Problems only began after he went through a difficult legal situation years later. The stress associated with ongoing court appearances triggered an inability to settle his body and mind, in the evenings.

He was amped up for several months on end and resorted to alcohol for a knockout effect. It worked for a short time however sleeping tablets + alcohol was needed now, to get even a partial result. The downsides of depressant drugs usually include side-effects and declined effectiveness with continued use.

He was frustrated with sleep and conflicted about whether to keep taking the tablets. Darren always kept them nearby, "just in case" he needed them. I asked if the tablets were currently working. He said, "No not really. Dammed if I do, dammed if I don't. The tablets occasionally lead to restful sleep however often it is as if I haven't taken anything at all."

Darren was stuck with an overactive sympathetic nervous system (stressed beyond what can be comfortably handled). The court case plus anxiety over sleep meant more cortisol stress hormone in his bloodstream. Medication can do only so much to reduce the effects of a stressful situation.

ALCOHOL AND SLEEP

One problem with overuse of alcohol is the suppression of REM sleep. This is a restorative part of our sleep cycle, for memory consolidation and emotional processing. Think about a tree that is overgrown with cluttered branches and old stems that are unnecessary. REM rest tidies up mind clutter. Although the actual processes are more complex, this simple analogy helps us understand.

Let's say I have emotional stress and I drink every night to push the feelings out of my awareness. After 6 months the issue that caused stress in the first place is still there. Furthermore, anxiety will convince my mind that I need alcohol to feel better, rather than healing the problem.

By drinking to avoid emotions I have three problems now. 1) The original issue is buried but still there, unresolved. 2) Alcohol is craved to continue escaping reality. 3) Alcohol will lower REM sleep quality. The effect of this is a lesser ability to deal with life and worsening stress from insomnia.

During the second half of the night sedative effects of alcohol wear off. A person might be thrust awake at 2:00am, unable to return to restful sleep. There may be dozens of micro-awakenings they aren't even aware of. Sleep becomes lighter. This contributes to mood disturbances and lethargy the day after drinking.

Regarding persistent disruptions to sleep, this can cause problems with anxiety, appetite, motivation and cognitive function. The point here is that regular alcohol use, **attempting to heal sleep**, is risky. I will be strong on this point. What is dangerous to body and mind is not a healing path, quite the opposite.

Risks of regular drinking are very high and rewards are minimal at best. We want our decisions to create better healing outcomes. Our choices need to create correction and satisfaction. Alcohol provides very little in these terms. Perhaps continued use of alcohol feeds anxiety rather than a true healing path, of mind and body (freeing us from burden).

I suggested that Darren needed better stress relief. After months of mental and emotional stress, we can use our body to become grounded rather than addicted.

LET'S GET PHYSICAL

We need a way to release the pressure inside. More time spent in our thinking and feeling zone, won't provide this. Alcohol cannot provide healing, so what can we do instead? Certain activities prompt the release of feel-good and stress relief chemicals such as serotonin, dopamine and oxytocin. By changing our internal chemistry, we start to feel much better.

Exercise is an opportunity to be grounded in your physical zone. The benefit of being grounded is to spend time out of your mental and emotional zones. In doing so, we shift our state. This is achieved by using our body. I know that when I hug loved ones, receive massage, swim in the ocean, play with pets, walk in nature and do tai chi my body chemistry will reward me.

There is the benefit of feeling good but also relaxation for body and mind. Instead of stressful cortisol brought on by worry and over-thinking, the body can be used to 'manually' create the desired feelings you want, and alter internal chemistry for health reasons.

Each person has their own preferred way to achieve grounding. The only condition should be that it is aligned for you. Choose a light or strenuous activity that you enjoy.

LIGHT ACTIVITIES:
Tai Chi
Stretching
Cooking
Darts

Water exercise
Being in nature
A short walk
Yoga Nidra
Osteopathy

STRENUOUS ACTIVITIES:
Dancing
Hiking
Bootcamp
Yoga Ashtanga
Weights and cardio
Rock climbing
Tennis, netball, soccer
Martial arts
Zumba

My job is to offer those like Elaine and Darren ways to influence their physiology. Getting grounded through exercise and activating the parasympathetic nervous system via hypnotherapy were 2 recommendations utilised with great effect.

If you are in 'stress mode' all day this is putting unfair pressure on your body. The alcohol and sleep medications will temporarily slow down the nervous system but will never be effective long-term in comparison to healing. We need ways to self-regulate – that is manage our mindset and emotions in healthy ways.

12 WAYS TO IMPROVE SLEEP NOW
Safety

Lock all doors and windows at night. The goal here is to make you safer and reduce worry. Securing your house achieves both these results. In an unlocked house it is likely the subconscious mind is more vigilant about strange noises. There is no advantage in trusting your neighbour's good nature, by leaving the house open.

BLANK TECHNIQUE

This technique was shared with me by a client. She said it cleared her mind in the evenings. While meditating before sleep, simply say the word "blank" in your mind. This can be timed with each inhale and exhale. Additionally, you could visualise a blank piece of paper, for a visual component.

FOOD

It is recommended to eat 3 regular sized portions per day and to finish more than 2 hours from bedtime. If your food plan isn't working, consider making adjustments that are satisfying. 80% of people with insomnia skip breakfast or/and lunch. A radical relationship with food impacts all our body's systems. Aim for moderation.

SLEEP SPACE

Make your bedroom aligned for sleep. Include calming colours and aromatherapy. Clean and organised is better than chaos. Clear out any loose items and pack clothes in the cupboard. Think 'bed room' not 'storage room.' Consider whether a TV is too stimulating for your sleep space.

JOURNAL WRITE

The benefit of journal writing is giving your thoughts and emotions a physical expression. Jot down on paper what is on your mind. Each evening write what happened, what you learnt and 5 things you are grateful for. In particular, letting your last thoughts be about gratitude before sleep, is highly recommended.

BEFORE SLEEP

Make your pre-sleep routine relaxing. 1 hour before bed is an opportunity to slow down body and mind. Reading and meditating are two such options for relaxation. Writing a to-do list ready for tomorrow can be useful too, as it takes away any need for your mind to remember everything while you are asleep.

AWAKE AT NIGHT
Finding oneself awake in the middle of the night is frustrating. If this happens to you focus on becoming physically very comfortable. Make sure the pillow and blanket weight are right for you. The philosophy here is that to be 'very comfortable' is winning the silver medal and brings you closer to sleep's gold.

SIGHTS
A room that is too bright or dim can interrupt sleep. There is no rule here except to make your bedroom the level of darkness you prefer. If blackout curtains to provide full darkness is needed, then that's okay. Conversely if leaving a light on helps you feel at ease, this too is fine. I would suggest that your night light be anything except a TV screen.

SOUNDS
Minimising nighttime sounds can take creativity. Road works, neighbours, animals, and snoring partners are a challenge. Some options include: Ear plugs, white noise such as a fan and pest removal of noisy critters. For snoring partners, send them to Inspire Hypnotherapy. I'll help them eat healthier and lose weight, so everyone sleeps better.

TEMPERATURE
An ideal sleep temperature is another category for personal preference. As a guide between 16 to 20 degrees Celsius (61 to 67 degrees Fahrenheit) is recommended. To regulate your comfort levels use air conditioners or heaters. Choose bedding and clothing that are comfortable for you.

CLEAN SHEETS
Don't underestimate the feeling of fresh linen to make your bed

inviting and pleasant. Clean sheets can add another level of comfort to your environment. Sweat, oils and skin can accumulate, so clean sheets provide a more hygienic and smooth sleeping surface. Psychologically, fresh bedding results in a positive mindset too.

WRITE YOUR SLEEP STATEMENT

"I wish my sleep to be easy, comfortable, dreamy, deeply nourishing, tranquil, automatic, long, peaceful, refreshing, still and effortless. My bedroom is an inviting and clean space. It is soft and clutter-free."

Use the words that align for you and read them each day.

TIME, MONEY AND ENERGY

THE CEO AND THE GRANDMOTHER

I met a gentleman, who ran two 8 figure companies. That same week I also met a retired grandmother. As it happened the grandmother was more stressed than the CEO, by quite a margin. She took on many tasks, which consumed nearly every hour of her day and night.

The CEO had responsibilities yet had streamlined his schedule. He was relaxed and according to him had, "Ample free time." As jobs came in, he completed them and delegated the excess to appropriate team members.

He received many requests each day and consciously said "no" as needed and is aware that taking on too much creates overwhelm. One tendency in life is to take on a maximum level of hard work, another is to use discernment to prioritise what we can comfortably fit in.

Using a conscious "yes" and "no" is valuable for all of us.

If saying yes to everything, his diary would be overloaded. He would be rushing to and from meetings and if one thing went wrong, problems would compound. He would be anxious trying to squeeze meetings too tightly together, all the while getting distracted by more tasks.

Is prioritising relevant for those not in an executive position? Yes 100%. Some of us are looking after a household, family, friendships and finances, physical as well as mental health. Leadership is applicable to every area of life. Ideally, we take care of responsibilities and allow time for quality of life and rewards.

MOIRA'S RETIREMENT

Taking care of her wheelchair bound husband was Moira's top priority. She also attended many social events, looked after grandchildren, volunteered for charitable causes and struggled with the cleaning and maintenance of their 2 packed properties and storage sheds. This grandmother said yes to nearly every task asked of her.

She filled most days from 6:00am-10:00pm, with activities but was supposed to be retired! Perhaps since not working she missed the structure that work provides. Stress bothered her and had recently gained 15kg. Looking after her own physical and mental health was lacking. When is there time for oneself while saying yes to everybody else?

This caring personality and do-it-alone style is not fair on Moira. She deserves rest and time for energy replenishment. Her household possessions hadn't been sorted by value in decades. Nothing was removed only more squeezed in. Moira's lifestyle was a reflection of her mental state. Say yes to more, and organise clutter later.

What does saying no to additional responsibility look like? Saying "no" doesn't mean "doing nothing." It means doing only the things that are worthwhile and trimming back what is not required. Prioritising need not be mean or rejecting of people either. We can take a short time to decide if someone's request is a "yes," "no" or "maybe later."

Strategies to improve Moira's time management:

- Not taking on new tasks
- Prioritising important tasks

- Getting support and delegating
- Slowing down over time
- Scheduling 1 day a week to unwind
- Allowing time to eat well

IS IT WORTH THE WEIGHT?

Note: If you have gained 15kg recently. Ask, "What emotional weight have I gained over the last 1-2 years? Is this added 'weight' above what can be managed?"

Saying no was not something Moira was comfortable with. Even when busy, she would keep approving more requests for her time. Being excessively busy is anxiety. It could be due to a belief that rest equals laziness or discomfort in simply being still. It could be guilt from childhood because a caregiver accused her of selfishness.

I believe our time can be used to create rewards for ourselves and others. When you don't feel very motivated it could be because what you are doing is not rewarding. When something saps our time, money, energy and peace of mind it is worth re-organising our lifestyle.

Busy without rest is extreme. Flexibility between yes and no is essential. You can discern between important, rewarding and unrewarding tasks. I have split types of tasks we have into 3 general categories. This helps us decide which tasks to approve and which to say no to.

Say, "Let me think about it," when someone requests you to take on more tasks. Then ask yourself privately, "Do I have the money, time and energy to take on more?"

PLANNING

To start planning your week, I suggest using a diary. If you don't have one, use a blank piece of paper. Just for this exercise, pretend that every task in your life is optional. Now, consciously fill in your diary. First schedule urgent and critical tasks, like picking up children from school and your job.

Next fill in all the rewarding activities you will do. These provide you with family fulfilment, money, energy, health, satisfaction, enjoyment, social connections, education and quality of life. Think about what rewarding means to you. Take forward action on what brings immediate fulfilment as well as investments that bring rewards over time.

Compound interest and exercise are 2 examples that produce rewards over time.

Once you have scheduled important and rewarding tasks in your diary, it is time to add down-time and rest. I am actually very pro-REST and pro-FUN. Once 80% of our day is stocked with worthwhile tasks, we can add healthy distractions and recreation.

I'm not a fan of getting rid of distractions 100%. They are a welcome break for the mind, used in moderation. I am a proponent of scheduling your distractions. Give yourself a whole hour to be distracted each day if suitable. Use this time to chill out, rest and consume content on your phone. When it is time to rest, enjoy. When it is time to work, do so decisively.

1) IMPORTANT TASKS

Take care of priorities and emergencies right away. If someone's well-being needs attention, we should take care of that. Time-sensitive tasks could include meeting an important deadline, legal obligations, critical care of people and honouring commitments.

In healthy self-esteem we take on two character traits. Number 1 is we are responsible for the results we get in life and honour our commitments. Number 2 is we let people know when they have deviated from their responsibilities. In doing so we can pass tasks back to the person who is meant to be doing it.

2) REWARDING TASKS AND OPPORTUNITIES

There are chances for us to experience great rewards. Being able to see and seize an opportunity is key. Someone might make a suggestion that is life changing. I have found that curiosity is very useful. Why is warm water so good for my metabolism? How do I invest in shares? What makes relationships truly rewarding?

With an open mind we discover something we didn't know before and can research to become more confident. Being open means we keep the door clear for potentially big opportunities, even if they are foreign to us. The curious mind pauses and explores an idea. Could this work for me?

1. A chance for higher education and learning new skills
2. The opportunity to travel, explore nature and different cultures
3. The chance for promotion or your dream job
4. An opportunity to start a business
5. The chance to invest and utilise compound interest
6. The opportunity to network and create relationships
7. An opportunity to start a family
8. The chance to focus on health, leading to improved energy and lower anxiety

3) DRAINING AND UNREWARDING TASKS

Finally, there are unimportant tasks that provide no reward. Pointless busywork, addictions, friends who cause drama, obsessive cleaning, taking on more when you are very tired. When the person, situation or job is not aligned with who you are and your goals, you can ditch or delegate to someone else.

Let go of tasks that rob your money, time and energy. Daily alcohol drinking, gambling, that friend you're weary of seeing every week, scrolling excessively on the phone and being guilted into taking on others problems. A situation doesn't have to be perfect. Just check that you aren't being robbed too dearly of the following:

- Energy

- Money
- Time
- Peace of mind

Think about the 4 categories listed above as currencies. When abundant in these areas we can happily give more and be charitable. It makes sense to serve when we are in credit. It can be done freely and without resentment. However, when low on money, time, energy and peace, we should be more self-serving.

A balance of giving and receiving is essential. Reflect on your own marriage and work agreements. The goal is an outcome of fairness between all parties. This is a very reasonable topic to have ongoing conversations about in your relationships.

TIME BLOCKS

The purpose of a time block is to be present with a single task for a period of time. It helps us separate from being pulled in multiple directions. A time block can be any length of time, although I would suggest making them between 30 minutes to 2 hours.

Being in work mode is satisfying. Being in rest mode in satisfying. Switching too quickly between them is ultimately chaotic and unrewarding. Using a time block means you get to engage wholly in what you are doing. Work gets done faster because there are fewer distractions and when relaxing, you can fully settle into that feeling.

It is unfortunate being pulled between exercise, family, work, emails, TV and social media all in a 30 minute block of time. I believe this is too much stimulation for the nervous system, resulting in anxiety. How can the mind truly settle when it knows we are shifting gears every two minutes?

If for example you are doing 30 minutes of yoga, it is very likely your phone notifications will buzz and beep, pulling you out of the present moment. We need a boundary that distractions cannot pass through. A barrier is enforced with action, like closing a door or putting your phone on silent.

Think about your nerves as little workers. Now, is each worker more balanced fulfilling one task, or bouncing quickly between several distractions? I am not saying that we will have zero stress. What is valuable though is to allow enough time for your nerves to settle into a steady rhythm.

Singular focus works better compared to fitting in a dozen things every hour. It really is enjoyable to be fully engaged with one experience.

PLAYING TENNIS WITH OUR COGNITIVE FUNCTION

Imagine a game of tennis. There is a tennis court, the net and a yellow ball. One half of the court represents action, work and solving problems. This is the Yang side, for getting things done. The other half represents slowing down, nurturing and switching off. This is the Yin side, for rest and energy replenishment.

The 'ball' can only be on the left or right side of the net. Likewise, you can only be in a **rest** or **action** space energetically but not both simultaneously. There is a clear distinction between the two sides.

In this metaphor pretend the ball is a person, bouncing back and forth between Yin and Yang, parasympathetic and sympathetic nervous system. Modern life has us back to the busy side, the minute we settle for some much-needed rest. We even joke and put this lifestyle on a pedestal to admire. "Look at me, I'm so busy multitasking!"

The mindfulness opportunity here is to stay on the nurturing side of the court long enough to benefit from it. Imagine you are settling into some worthwhile relaxation. Then from across the other side of the net is a family problem, household chores and your phone. They are all stimulating activities (Yang), that we think we have to jump back into.

Half working and half resting don't fully achieve either objective. Decide which side of the court to be on and create a time block that is dedicated to one thing. Block out a period of 30 minutes minimum to be fully present with a single task.

Scheduling work and rest separately means you can truly enjoy both.

Enjoy the Yin side of the court. When resting be fully in that energy. Collect your thoughts and rest your body. This is a time to choose a relaxing hobby, cuddling pets, music or nature. Meditation, deep breathing and gratitude rituals are also aligned with Yin energy.

And when you are working be fully in that Yang energy. Enjoy being productive and completing tasks. Exercise outside and workouts at the gym are action based too. Yang is useful to make things happen (not thinking about doing something however completing it). Action makes what we think come true.

TIME BLOCK OPPORTUNITIES

- Morning 30-60 minutes. Prepare for the day with self-care, body movement, water, breakfast and whatever brings you vitality. Check your phone after the time block has ended.
- Lunch 30-60 minutes. Use this time block to give your body and mind a break. Collect your thoughts, stretch your legs, eat and rest.
- Evening 30-60 minutes. Use the time after dinner to slow down. Self-nurturing, light reading, meditation and a gratitude ritual are options. Turn your phone off in preparation for sleep.

THE CASE FOR BOTH YIN AND YANG

Check that your lifestyle includes a balance of Yin and Yang. Action and planning, exercise and recovery, tension and calm, work and play, fast and slow, serving others and self-nurture time. These pairs of opposites complement each other, ultimately leading to greater satisfaction in life. Not missing half of what you need however getting enough of these valuable energies.

When becoming too extreme, in either Yin or Yang, people often say "I am out of balance." What does out of balance really mean? Being removed from the middle ground. Living life at full blast, or being overly passive, are far away from the middle.

The solution is to satisfy the left/right, Yin/Yang equation. In mathematics a solved equation has one side = to the other. In terms of mental health and anxiety reduction, a healthy balance of Yin and Yang is essential. Be sure to include both throughout your week.

REPAIRMAN

A gentleman I consulted with had his own handyman business, working 14 hour days. Chris did his job, put the kids to bed at night, then crashed himself. There was no time for eating until the very end of day. Others care was very high. This imbalance manifested as having secret takeaway on the way home and then a full dinner cooked by his wife an hour later. His weight increased and energy decreased, as he had taken on too much.

Note: Energy decreases when our digestion system is overworked. A recommended portion size is slightly more than the volume of your fist loosely closed. Why? This is the size of your stomach. Chris was eating 2 burgers and a home cooked meal, which was about 3 stomachs worth of food in total. It is recommended to spread your meals out over a few sittings, which means easier digestion.

Chris and I chatted and put ideas in place to help him find balance. He would now enjoy a full half an hour break around lunch-time. This way Chris is taking rest for himself and will not be starving for food at the end of day. He utilised this break to eat and organise afternoon tasks. He took a little time for himself, cut out the takeaway meal and after 12 weeks reported a weight loss of 10kg.

1. One ½ hour break
2. Eating breakfast and lunch, so not over-hungry at night
3. Cut out the evening takeaway meal

I mentioned, "By the way if you are in small business and booked out 14 hours a day with appointments, raise your prices. A 12%

increase means you can earn the same amount with 90 minutes free time per day (7.5 hours per week). That's working smarter, not harder. Minus the 5x 30 minute lunch breaks and that's still earning the same money with 5 hours saved per week.

- Gets rest to replenish energy
- Eating better leading to weight loss
- Valuing his time
- Less stress

DECISIONS

Ahead is a framework you can use to make better decisions. This is not what I think you should do but how to determine for yourself what is best. Some decisions carry greater risk, so protecting oneself is important. Other options provide so much benefit, with little risk, it is worth grasping the opportunity.

Logic can be used to weigh the pros and cons of the path ahead. This can be cross-checked by your gut instinct. Let's say there are plenty of pros, but something *feels* wrong. Your instinct may be picking up on an unspecified danger. Utilise both practical logic and your inner guidance when taking the next step.

If you have trouble making a decision, list all of the likely upsides and possible risks. For larger decisions take your time and trust your gut instinct. Seeking advice from loved ones and professionals can help you gain different perspectives. The best outcome is one that saves time, money and energy.

LOWER RISK DECISIONS

Action is one of the foundations of mastering anxiety, as opposed to avoidance. Mental activity and overanalysing won't bring us any peace. Worrying uses energy but there is no physical expression to release the mind.

Anxiety about uncertain outcomes is resolved by making a

decision. When the choice is made, we free up mental space. My suggestion when deciding between alternatives, is to pick the new option. You can't know for sure something is right for you without experiencing it first. This is applicable for low-risk decisions, where the stakes are minimal.

Affirmation: "When I make a decision and act, I set my thoughts free. I won't keep them prisoner any longer."

You don't need to be attached to a job or situation when you are deeply dissatisfied, on a daily basis. If change is needed then explore your options. When goals are aligned with your values you can move forward with confidence.

IS LEAVING A TERRIBLE JOB LOW RISK?

Let's say the current job pays 30% less than the industry average, drains energy, the staff have low standards and is far from home. Getting almost any other job will be better if the present one is not rewarding. Seeking employment that aligns with who we are and fulfils our needs, greatly improves circumstances.

The current job has several downsides, costing money, energy, peace of mind and time. It is worth applying for something else because the value of the current job is significantly low. We minimise risk in this example by accepting new employment, before leaving the old workplace.

Be tactical in decision making. To remain secure don't give up current employment until a contract is signed with a new company. Keep your present job while looking for another that has several potential upsides. A change that is close to home, suits you better, pays more and has great culture, is an improvement.

HIGHER RISK DECISIONS

Moving house, health treatments and selecting a romantic partner are choices with high stakes. The most reliable way to reduce worry, is to gain as much information as possible. When we covered job interview confidence earlier in this book, we discovered that turning up unprepared was nerve-wracking. On the other hand, gaining information before and during the interview gives us a basis from which to build true confidence.

When stakes are higher, like, "Is this the right house to buy?" be very thorough. Make slow decisions about things that will impact your long-term future. Gather maximum information when making big decisions.

Meet with a mortgage broker, visit your bank, meet with several real estate agents, attend open houses on weekends, get a maintenance history, a house inspection, chat with friends who are homeowners, join online groups about buying property, listen to podcasts about the housing market and seek quality advice from an independent financial advisor.

Spend time gathering information and weighing pros and cons. The more knowledge you get, the more certain you will be. For high impact decisions make sure the deal is fair and have a backup plan. It may be wise not to put all of your eggs in a single basket. Confidence with investing comes after gaining knowledge.

Think about a decision you are mulling over. Can you research what is needed yourself? Would a phone call, email or text to an appropriate person save you time and worry? See if you can increase knowledge to heal the unknowns you have.

FINANCIAL RISK HYPOTHETICAL

When 'new money' enters our bank account well-meaning people will tell you what to use it for. I say this with no judgement but majority have not studied finances nor have experience investing. There are a few considerations to be aware of if you have experienced a sudden increase in your wealth. Money is valuable so we want to protect it.

Let's examine the thought process about how to invest $100,000. In this hypothetical someone has just received an inheritance from a dear loved one, now passed away. The person has no other savings and earns enough wage to cover general living expenses.

They are given two options for investing their money.

Option 1) Use the $100,000 for a 20% deposit on a $500,000 house. Family members tell them that buying property is a safe and worthwhile investment for the long term. They are right about property being relatively safe and lucrative but the 100K is all the money this person has. There will be ongoing costs associated with maintenance and insurance. If there are interest rate rises the mortgage might become unaffordable.

If this person had other assets and a higher income, then this deal would be safer. Additional resources and a partner to combine with, would add more layers of cushion (safety). Invest in ways that you are comfortable with, not near the edge of ruin. We don't want to invest all of our money without cushions to fall back on.

Option 2) Invest in a new company that has nearly doubled their profits every month for the last 3 months. This offer has come through a friend who is a partner in the business. They have solid financial backing and it looks like they will keep growing. Expected return in 2 years could be $750,000 they say.

They are asking for $100,000, the exact amount that was inherited. The potential for reward is there, however so are the risks. The amount to invest is 100% of their money. It is too risky to invest everything we own in one thing. The business could easily be successful or closed in 2 years. No one knows for sure.

Why are they asking an inexperienced investor in the first place? This puts one at too high a risk. What if the only reason they are doubling profits is because new investors keep pumping money into the scheme?

I personally know several people that put all of their money into one business deal and lost every single dollar within a year. If you have recently been blessed with 'new money' hold onto it for 6 months, work on increasing your income, then slowly start to invest a small percentage of your money in an asset that you are knowledgeable about.

Move slowly at first with new money, then act decisively armed with knowledge.

Anyone wanting you to make a **fast decision** about your valuable money, will cause you to quickly lose the lot. Financial decisions are to be made slowly, with due diligence. We weigh up the pros and cons ourselves to determine risk and reward. Let the vultures fly away and find some other sucker to scavenge from. Say, "Not today vulture!"

Neither the house nor business deal, have the risk to reward ratio right. With these two options put to the side now, here is what I would do in this person's position. This is not financial advice but something to form your own conclusions about.

I would implement a cushions strategy. The purpose of cushions are that even if you fall, your landing will be soft. I would put 20% into a bank account earning interest that can be easily accessed. I would put another 20% into a term deposit earning higher interest. 50% into top Australian and American shares. The remaining 10% could go into the technology industry, which has higher reward and risk however there are cushions to fall back on.

By spreading out the money there is no single point of failure. The high risk of putting money into just one investment is gone and there remains opportunity for growth. Having only 10% go into a risky asset, takes care of the most important thing, protecting the majority of your money from massive loss.

INCREASING ENERGY

Life is better with the energy and health to enjoy life. The following ideas are designed to work with your holistic health in mind. What does that mean? The tactics will make you feel good, increase energy and are aligned with body wellness.

DRINKING WATER

2-3 litres of water daily is very advantageous. Muscles and organs, including the brain become hydrated. This means greater mental clarity. 1 litre first thing in the morning will awaken your energy. Have hot for a metabolism boost and to aid in weight control. Drink in the form you enjoy most, whether it be still or sparkling.

SUPPLEMENTS

A supplement is holistic when providing the body what it is deficient in. If a blood test reveals a vitamin or mineral is lacking, this is worth correcting. There are several vitamins that are correlated with energy, mood and wellness. Check that your B12, Vitamin C, Vitamin D, Iron and Magnesium are at acceptable levels.

EASIER DIGESTION

When recovering from chronic fatigue the best thing I did was change what I ate. Namely, reducing portions of foods heavy on digestion. If feeling tired after eating, consider lessening portions of bread, dairy, processed sugar, red meat, soft drinks and alcohol. The harder your body works, the more energy is lost digesting.

ENERGY BOOST

Be aware of what makes you come alive and boosts energy. Have fun and do what you love. It's not all boring health stuff and hard work. Enjoy the beach, hiking, laughing, dancing, playing games, spending time with kids. Activities outdoors immerse you in something called negative ions, particularly by the sea and rainforest. These charged particles create positive feelings in you biochemically.

MEDITATION

When tired or anxious the body is more likely to be in fight/flight mode. Meditation activates the parasympathetic nervous system and reduces cortisol. When relaxed you are more likely to replenish your energy reserves. Meditation can aid in sleep preparation too, calming body and mind prior to bedtime.

Your body knows how to operate at its peak. Give it a helping hand and it will help you back.

TIME, MONEY AND ENERGY CONCLUSION

Time is a currency traded for what we value. One who has lots to do however enjoys what they spend time on, doesn't mind being busy. We can't create nor destroy time however can use it for worthwhile and rewarding goals. Building a life that is rewarding is my favourite definition of time mastery. This includes being satisfied and not burnt out.

Deciding how to use our time, money and energy, can make the difference between getting the most out of life or overwhelm. Consider the following with how you spend your valuable time:

- Fill each day with important, rewarding and self-nurturing activities
- Don't be rushed into making decisions. Take time to determine risk and reward
- Let go of anything that robs too much peace of mind, money, time and energy
- Peace of mind, money, time and energy are worth protecting
- Use time blocks to create separation between work and rest
- Using the stopwatch function on your phone can help set a time block
- For small decisions, act fast so you can move forward
- For large decisions, include thorough planning, seek advice and weighing your options
- Any requests for your time can be scrutinized by filter. I will take care of urgent. I will work on rewarding, family, health and financial tasks. Unrewarding shall not pass through my gate

BALANCED LIFESTYLE

The purpose of a balanced mindset is to see clearly what is true. Thinking realistically means we will be more prepared to deal with challenges. If for example I am very optimistic, I might be surprised when life doesn't work out. And if I am very pessimistic, I might not even bother trying to set goals. The middle ground is a balanced, true perspective of a situation. This will reveal itself over the coming pages.

Being able to consider the positives and negatives, advantages and drawbacks of a situation is empowering. We are less likely to be anxious. Instead, we will be well prepared and resilient.

A lifestyle that is too busy or sedentary is stressful. Balancing activity and recovery is valuable. It's tempting to dream of a life of comfort and pleasure but overindulgence causes stress too. Human beings thrive with a balance of support and challenge, work and rest, fast and slow, obligation and reward, eating and digestion, planning and action.

CAREER BALANCE

It may be that you currently work just for money. This is practical but sacrifices being satisfied. When work has a balance of effort and reward, then life is better. A job can be much more than a paycheque.

25% of our lives are spent working, making it one of the most important parts of our lifestyle.

Health and immune system will be stronger. Anxiety about going to a terrible job won't be there. Your earnings will be higher at a job you like, because of lower chances of quitting and getting fired. You are more likely to get promoted into roles you are skilled at.

At a job that is enjoyable, with low stress, there will be no need to binge on food, alcohol and drugs after work. There is no need to escape from a career you like. You will find yourself to be steadier rather than feeling bi-polar (having anxious ups and downs each week).

This is the power of alignment. When something is right for you, emotional volatility lessens. The nervous system gets used to being steady. Be real about the advantages and disadvantages of the job you have currently, and the one you want. Check if the conditions are a match with what you need.

The average person changes career 5-7 times in their life. What you do in your twenties might not be the same as in your forties. Each time you make a job change, ensure it is in alignment with the value you like expressing to the world.

Every job is worthwhile however it is worth finding one that is right for you. Reflect on how in alignment you are with your career.

- Are you passionate or interested in the job you have?
- Does it provide you with money, time, energy, peace or other rewards?
- Are you able to express your values and beliefs at work?
- Are your skills and talents on display in your current role?

CAREER POSITIVES:
Helping people
    Receiving income
    Feeling significant
    Using your talents

Expressing yourself
Making friends
Gaining new skills
Holiday/sick pay
Stable routine
Certainty

CAREER NEGATIVES:

Mentally drained
Physically tired
Time away from family
Time away from what you love
Workplace conflict
Long commutes to and from work
Overwhelm
Hot and cold work environments
Not recognised for talents
Putting yourself last

Every career has positives and negatives. There are costs and rewards. A career that is too emotionally volatile can take a toll physically and mentally. When the costs of a particular job outweigh the rewards, this is when we consider making a change for the better. Choose work that is aligned and fulfilling to you.

BODY BALANCE

"I love my body because it helps me fulfil my purpose."

A person's physical appearance is put under the most scrutiny and becomes linked to self-worth. Judgement as unfortunate as it is, is common. The shape, colour, length, width, depth and other variables are unique but never bad.

- Age young or old
- Skin light or dark
- Skin rough or smooth
- Height tall or short
- Body shape wide or slim
- Hair little or much
- Eyes apart or narrow
- Eyebrows bushy or sparse
- Genitals large or small
- Breasts large or small
- Muscles large or small
- Belly button innie or outie
- Features under or overrepresented

Many people enjoy larger features on a lady, man or alternate gender. Many people enjoy shorter features. Many people enjoy slim, firm, rough, soft or smooth features. Many enjoy hairy and wild features. Many enjoy a body with rare and unusual features. Every unique body is saying, "Love me for who I am."

There are people that will enjoy your exact features. I am certain there are people who enjoy my uniqueness whereas others prefer a point of difference. My life is best lived not trying to please all people but primarily myself and a few others.

A pivot from pleasing others to pleasing myself has greatly reduced body-related anxiety. It is not enough for 'everyone' and 'society' but it's enough for 'me.' In truth my body is slim, and quirky and it is also strong, responsive and sexy. Appreciating all of my traits, even the ones I didn't originally like, is self-acceptance.

Over time the body changes. Certain features become more or less expressed. Bones, muscles, skin, genitals, hair and other characteristics transform, and that's okay. It is our job to continuously love our body as it expands and contracts. Every change has blessings.

A baby has awareness of their physical world but not self-acceptance, nor self-rejection. Judgement is something that we learn and use it to fit in with someone else's criteria of what is enough. When I say that pleasing ourselves is most important, this is because everybody has their own version of beautiful. It is extreme pressure to please 8 billion or even 8 people.

We must teach ourselves and others that no 'body' is positive or negative. Only anxious judgement makes it appear so. Simply, the body is, 'the body that it is.' Each body helps the owner fulfil their purpose on this Earth. Our body is great as it is. We start to believe this by making self-appreciation a daily habit.

BODY BLESSINGS

Going bald for men is natural and provides blessings. Less hair is a sign of getting older. Looking mature can be useful at work. In many cases it is beneficial, showing that you are experienced. You'll save money due to no longer needing shampoo, conditioner or haircuts. There is a time saving too. No need for brushing and styling.

Scars can be distressing and are also a blessing. A medical scar can represent healing and survival. The body is marked because it allowed doctors to heal your body. "Thank you broken ribs which stopped injury to my heart and lungs. Thank you, symptoms, which revealed an underlying problem that got treated saving my life. Thank you scars for allowing healing to take place."

Start to view body changes in not just an anxious way but including the healing context. See the truth that your body is blessed, functional and complex. It's worth appreciating the benefits of the body you have now, instead of what you used to have or might have in the future.

Healing the relationship with your body is a present moment act of love. "I am in the body I am in." There is no other body to love except your beautiful body here and now. Find the blessing in all that you are.

PHYSICAL HEALTH POSITIVES:
Longevity
- Abundant energy
- Sleep well
- Better mood
- Better digestion
- Relaxed nervous system
- Less inflammation and pain
- Mobility
- Endurance
- Freedom

PHYSICAL HEALTH NEGATIVES:
Takes effort
- Time to prepare food
- Time to learn about health
- Body sore from exercise
- Money spent on supplements
- Going into surgery
- Trying to find healthy options
- Effort and discipline
- Less connection with unhealthy friends
- Rejecting people who were a bad influence
- (like smoking, drinking and drug associates)

MONEY BALANCE

To say we don't care about money is avoidance. To be greedy with money is obsession. However, to view money realistically and use it for a purpose, is recommended. Finances are a major part of life and being empowered gives greater ability to control our own circumstances.

Being empowered does not equate to greediness. A means to survive and take care of loved ones could never be called greedy. This is essential. There is no benefit to avoiding what money provides, including, the ability to travel, get health care, education and contributing to people in ways that are meaningful.

Be wary of people whose mindset are excessively lacking or greedy. Getting a fair deal at home and work is balanced. This means you get a reasonable reward for your contribution. The more responsibility you take for results, the more you should receive. Building a healthy self-esteem ensures we don't just give it all away, we invest in ourselves first.

MONEY POSITIVES:

Get out of financial hardship
  No longer having to rely on others
  Proud to achieve financial independence
  Use money to make more money
  Choice of where to live
  Choice of where to work
  Ability to afford education/tutor for kids
  Provide for family and friends
  Have backup security money when needed
  Have enough for fun, travel, recreation and expression

MONEY NEGATIVES:

Can divide family and friends
  Can be tired working so much
  Takes effort to learn the money game
  Takes effort to protect money
  Stress being in a higher tax bracket
  More complicated tax returns
  Meetings with financial advisors and accountants
  Dealing with losses in property, shares and business
  Need updated security
  Target for theft

Keeping money consists of investing in assets, protecting those assets, purposeful spending, increasing income, getting tax advice, marketing yourself, knowledge, diversification, insurance, avoiding scams, beating inflation and other systems. In short, it takes planning and effort.

Wealth likes certainty, self-worth and structure.

Be aware of any conflicting beliefs that could be affecting your relationship with money. Let's say I want wealth but call money accumulators evil. I also say it is better to give than receive and am critical of those who are abundant. How could I possibly gain lots of something I believe is evil? Is it possible to achieve wealth while feeling guilty in the process?

The chances are high of remaining just over broke (less than 4 weeks of survivability without income). The solution to money judgement is to stop putting extreme labels on it. Filter out money beliefs that are false. Think in terms of truth and balance. The truth is always more empowering than an anxious-false-reality.

Money Judgements:
Wealthy people are good
    Wealthy people are evil
    Money is good
    Money is evil

Money Reality:
Money can be exchanged
    Money gives us more options
    Money has positives and negatives
    Money simply is

TRAVEL BALANCE

Travel is a favourite escape for many types of people. It is a chance to get away from work and see unique places around the world. Does travel ever go perfectly, without discomfort? When travelling is there only happiness, or an enhancement of highs and lows?

I love travelling to islands and taking pictures while snorkelling. The moments I have experienced in nature are some of my favourite memories. I have swum with sharks, seen fish leaping out of the water in front of me and had close encounters with turtles, squid, eels and tropical marine life.

While there were great times, there is always a counter-balance. For every high, an inevitable low. For every wow, an unfortunate ouch! Here are several: Sunburn, bitten by sandflies, water that is very cold, cuts and scrapes from rocks, dehydration and tiredness. Swimming back to shore alone at dusk is another memorable downside. Several minutes in the water with no visibility, at a time when sharks are most active was not pleasant.

TRAVEL LIFESTYLE

There was a time prior to C-19 when many Influencers were showing off the travel lifestyle. It looked very appealing to run a business from your laptop in Europe, Bali or South America. They enjoyed freedom to work and relax as they pleased.

In 2020, when international travel was all but halted, these influencers found themselves stuck overseas or having to pay 1 year's salary for a flight home. What started out as a lifestyle of freedom became very restrictive.

I mention examples like these, so we are prepared for the inevitable counter-balance. Freedom and restriction occur together. As do comfort and discomfort, easy and hard, fast and slow, connection and disconnection.

A balanced, real view of travel means you can enjoy yourself and also prepare for what comes your way. The higher mind knows that every experience will have its positives and negatives. Expecting reality to occur is empowering. This is the opposite of anxiety.

Those who are willing to endure the highs and lows, do so, because travel is valuable to them. Even if someone says to a traveller, it could be dangerous, they will still go. They are aware of the risks and have determined it is worth it.

TRAVEL POSITIVES:
Cultural experiences
  Memories for a lifetime
  Connection with people
  Connection with nature
  Expanded awareness
  Swimming, walking and sightseeing
  Relaxation in the sun
  Break from work
  Food experiences
  Adventure and education

TRAVEL NEGATIVES:
Airline delays and jetlag
  Cramped seating
  Packing and unpacking
  Dehydration, exhaustion
  Getting sick
  Getting lost
  Financial costs
  Robbed/lost luggage
  Stuck with difficult people
  Extreme heat and cold

SEX BALANCE
Imagine meeting someone who has dozens of sex rules. Must do it at

this time of day and only with certain conditions. Will only display sexual affection after several months getting to know each other. Many rules can take away the spontaneity. Someone who is very rigid might be denying their natural desires, in order to feel secure.

Now imagine meeting someone with an opposite attitude. They say they have been with hundreds of partners and believe in free love. They want to be sexually active, even after just a short time of knowing each other. We might have to check they are responsible, whether they have an STD and what the boundaries are. Someone who is extremely free, satisfies their sexual urges but lacks care for the consequences of their actions.

Back in my drug taking phase I recall two friends who had sex after a night of taking ecstasy. Should have been all pleasure, right? The next morning they said it wasn't even very good. Like they scratched an itch physically but that was it. One of them was ridden with guilt too because they had just cheated on their partner.

Both expression and restraint have a place. That's balanced. Trust does not need reduce sexual excitement though. Trust helps couples deepen their expression over time. Whilst no sexual partner will be perfect, find someone that is a right fit for you. Check that communication is open. Work on clear boundaries as well as opportunities to go with the flow, with a trusted and aligned person.

A healthy sex life includes communication between partners. Discovering each other's desires can mean being vulnerable. This is scary and exciting. Embracing both emotions can elevate sexual experiences beyond a couple that has repressed emotions. Let your partner know your comfort level and what you would like to explore.

The greatest blessing that comes from sex, is life. Creating a new human is one of the greatest responsibilities and rewards we can experience. There are many positives ranging from pleasure, to creating life. A healthy relationship with sex is realistic, keeping in mind there are downsides (pleasure and pain always remaining in balance).

SEX POSITIVES:

Pregnancy hormones
    Creating a family
    Vulnerability leading to intimacy
    Connection
    Excitement
    Bliss
    Orgasm
    Release and relaxation
    Pleasurable sensations
    Transcendental experiences

SEX NEGATIVES:

Pregnancy hormones
    Uncomfortable sex
    Painful during or after
    Side effects of contraception drugs
    Vulnerability, leading to hurt feelings
    Feeling disconnected
    Pressure to 'perform'
    Cheating partners
    Tired afterwards
    Misunderstandings and rejection

TECHNOLOGY BALANCE

Wise technology use can empower you. Modern products and services make life easier in many cases, like medical devices, GPS (global positioning system), financial apps, electric wheelchairs and many more I won't mention here. A moderate use of technology is recommended.

Under-using technology, like not having WIFI or an email address is limited. This might look like still driving to the bank to withdraw $500. Next stop is the post office, lining up to pay a bill

HEALING ANXIETY

in cash. Total time 60 minutes, rather than using internet banking, which takes 2 minutes.

Over-using technology looks like using your phone sitting on the toilet. Later in the living room using a laptop, while watching TV and scrolling your mobile phone. Then having meals with family yet still scrolling social media and answering work emails. Extreme technology use results in craving stimulation through mobile apps at the expense of being present with anyone or anything else.

The moderate technology user spends time on their electronic device for a purpose. Then they put it aside. When it is time to work, they do so. And when it is time to play with the kids, they can be present. Often technology is used to stimulate our senses. This urge can be highly addictive, causing physical and mental distress.

Over stimulation by technology causes our brain to process information fast yet forget just as quickly. I can remember the plot and quotes from movies decades ago. Compare this to watching 100 short videos on a phone. I can remember only a fraction and could not quote anything from this short content.

Consuming high levels of information through technology will disrupt mood and energy levels.

Over time focus is lessened and memory fragmented. Anxiety will get worse due to a highly stimulated nervous system. Consider moving to slower paced entertainment. Watching a movie then having a break from all devices is reasonable. Reading or listening to an audio book is slower too, allowing us to consume and integrate the content.

At my most extreme I used to check social media and work accounts at 3 o'clock in the morning. I was actually bored being asleep. My mind was looking for reward and stimulation. Be aware of compulsion and addiction to use technology, particularly at night. Without care it can creep into every area of our lives.

Thankfully there are several ways to care for an over-stimulated nervous system. Choose a grounding ritual that doesn't require technology to be involved, like being in nature or meditation. Exercise outdoors is another helpful activity for body and mind. You get the benefit of body movement, being outside and it is grounding for your nervous system.

Remember to look after your children and teenagers. This is the first generation that falls asleep with a mobile phone in their hand. Do what it takes to protect their developing brains.

For those who want to reduce their technology use, decide on times to use it and times you will not. Some even have their home WIFI completely off between 10pm and 6am, to create a healthy balance.

Positives of Technology:

Can be lifesaving
- Convenient, saves time
- Makes life easier
- Increased standard of care
- Increased comfort
- Access to empowering information
- Can be used to make money
- Online tutorials
- Solves problems
- Connection around the world

Negatives of Technology:

Can be expensive
- Can rob us of time
- Caught in online scams
- Disrupting sleep quality
- Technology addiction
- Affects our energy and mood

Managing dozens of online accounts
Loss of connection close to home
Can distract from family
Over-reliance

FOOD BALANCE

I was asked by a client, "How can I know which food to be free with and which to restrict."

My answer: "Remember a Christmas celebration when there was excessive consumption. And think about a time when there was too little to eat, like a calorie-controlled diet or difficult times growing up. Neither of these are balanced. Focus on the middle ground, satisfaction brought about by real food and reasonable portions."

- Satisfaction is achieved by a meal you enjoy and fulfils your hunger. Neither under-eating nor over-eating is recommended. It is possible to look after ourselves physically, mentally and emotionally. This means living a moderate path that minimises stress to your digestion and nervous system.
- Eating beyond physical hunger is indulgence. After people have lived a lifestyle of restriction, they bounce to the other extreme, binging. Comfort foods like, sugar, dairy, bread, chips and snacks, ironically make us feel uncomfortable. Signs of excess include: heaviness, bloated, tiredness, inflammation and anxiety.
- Under-eating is a form of restriction. Tasteless food and denying the body what it needs is too sacrificial. Willpower lasts a short time and you'll find yourself back to binging afterwards. Signs of restriction include: unfulfilled, demotivated, food always on the mind and battling with willpower.

Moderation can provide a healing path, focused on satisfying physical hunger. Sure, food can still be pleasurable BUT it is not the primary motivation. As we know, overusing foods as a treat will make us anxious. Moderation means we hear our body wisdom and make corrections.

When you are balanced, relationship with food is judgement-free and anxiety-free. Think in terms of cause and effect. When we see that certain foods cause certain outcomes. I can tell you that addiction is more likely present, when the person has an imbalanced view, labelling foods either positive or negative, black or white, good or bad.

I used to eat chocolate snacks every day. Chocolate cookies, chocolate or chocolate cookies dipped in chocolate. So basically chocolate. I was seeking the pleasure and stress release they provided. The downsides were that I developed fatigue, digestion problems and anxiety, which the sugar contributed to.

> *Every comfort food is also a discomfort food.*

I didn't want to change. My mind wanted its pleasure and nothing would slow down my habit. Well, the reality of declining physical health stopped me. The end result of using food to stimulate serotonin and dopamine, was a period of chronic fatigue. There is always a slow-down, after prolonged stimulation.

- A diet including meat can be balanced with fresh vegetables
- Busy lifestyles can be balanced with self-nurturing and recovery
- Aim for physical satisfaction from food
- Avoid being over-hungry and over-full

A mindfulness technique I run through with every client is noticing the physical effect of each food type. They become aware of any foods that cause symptoms like tiredness, indigestion and heaviness. Often too much bread or dairy are the culprits. We then incorporate more meals that promote easy digestion and are satisfying.

"~~Eat everything in moderation.~~"

"Purposefully eat foods that are right for you."

One of the key reasons we observe positive and negative food traits, is that it safeguards against addiction. You can't be obsessed with a balanced point-of-view. What this looks like practically is being calm about food. No food is good or bad, just like you are not good or bad. We can simply observe the effect of our actions and choose what aligns for our well-being

The truth is 'good' and 'bad' traits occur together. This gives you the whole picture, or what we call a balanced perspective.

Food Positives:
Tasty
- Pleasure
- Essential for life
- Connected to the Earth
- Flavour combinations
- Shared with family and friends
- Provides energy
- Hydrating
- Provides minerals and vitamins
- Anti-inflammatory (healing foods and teas)

Food Negatives:
Intolerances
- Allergies
- Costs money
- Time consuming
- Reflux and bloating
- Food poisoning
- Over-full causing sleep trouble
- Food cravings
- Food disorders
- Inflammatory (processed foods and alcohol)

BALANCED VIEW OF GENTLE AND TOUGH LOVE

Being kind is a philosophy for many. The intention is to be heart centred and compassionate with others. Whilst kindness is useful in general, certain situations require a stronger approach. Being a leader at work, parenting children and negotiating relationship agreements are examples where firmness is often needed.

Note: I am not in favour of extreme softness or extreme hardness.

Love in action can be strong, clear, empowered and holding people to being accountable. If one person is not receiving what is deserved or promised, that's taking advantage. Love can stand up for what is right and this takes strength and volume.

PASSIVE, HARSH OR ASSERTIVE

Bec mentioned that confidence was low when communicating with authority figures. If there is a risk of hurting someone's feelings, Bec becomes passive. Those who try to be 100% kind, are afraid of conflict. They are keeping the peace outwardly however *the battle goes inward* knowing they deserve better treatment. A fair deal.

She wished for the ability to stand her ground and state needs clearly. Bec had given notice to leave a business rental and left the place in good condition. She expected to receive bond money back (4 weeks rent), but the landlord was not releasing the cash. Furthermore, he was communicating disrespectfully.

My guess was the landlord uses intimidation to discourage people from pursuing what is rightfully theirs. Bec believes that people will do the right thing, given the chance. Granted, most of the time they will however on other occasions there are characters who take advantage of a passive nature for personal gain. Taking legal action to hold people accountable, has a place.

I possess a voice. It will be heard.

I asked Bec if she would like her 2 daughters to learn the value of standing their ground. "Would it be empowering for your daughters to get fair treatment? Would a firm 'yes' and a firm 'no' be useful going forward in life? The yes says they are certain of what they want. The no says I will not be a pushover."

Me continued: "Would it be valuable to say 'no' to their future boyfriends, partners, employers and employees, if necessary? Would there be downsides always going along with what others want? Would holding people true to their word in business and family be an okay thing to teach your daughters? Would there be times when authentically standing up for themselves is essential?"

Bec: "Oh yes there would!!!"

This lit a fire in Bec and she knew that standing up for fair is an example she would like to set for her girls.

Even if a business partner, co-worker or landlord is taken aback, you haven't done anything wrong by requesting what is rightfully yours. Feelings are important but fair treatment is more important. We should not be kind while someone is taking advantage of us. The landlord's high self-esteem and harsh behaviour needs to be humbled.

In fact, if someone guilts you for standing your ground then, they don't respect your boundary and are manipulating, to get what they want. They are expecting you to be passive, while their exaggerated sense of self continues recklessly.

Make decisions based on fairness.

Bec found that when approaching a new situation, confidence was lower compared to normal. She wondered, "Why is confidence not there in dealing with the landlord? Could I get more information? Am I lacking knowledge?" She and I discussed the strategies that build confidence.

Bec got support through the discussion with me. Afterwards she acquired legal knowledge regarding the lease agreement, which gave her confidence. A follow-up email was sent to the landlord with no fear and got the money she was owed, within 20 minutes. Confidence increases with support, knowledge and action based on fairness.

Remember that being strong is not abusive. Assertively requesting a fair deal is not harsh. Having our needs heard and understood is reasonable, even if other people don't like it. Anxiety is scared to ask for what is right. Love stands up for fairness, equality and truth.

- Was Bec Passive? No.
- Was she Harsh? No.
- Did she get empowered with knowledge? Yes.
- Did she assertively request fairness and humble the entitled character? Yes.

BALANCED EMOTIONS

Emotions are expressions of our beliefs, even if we aren't always conscious of those beliefs. The extent that I believe something is positive or negative, good or bad, right or wrong, the more intense the emotion will be.

Perception impacts how we feel, even more than circumstances. It is worth examining judgemental tendencies that are tangled in anxiety then guide our mindset back to healing. Check if your judgements are accurate. See if you have all the facts or need to gather more data before making conclusions.

If an emotion prompts you to reflect on beliefs, this is useful.

Intense emotions are trying to 'wake us up to reality.' It is a worthy goal to make our beliefs empowering, useful and true. It is possible to make our feelings less intense and shorter in duration. By taking control of our thinking and beliefs, emotions can become balanced.

Remember that a synonym of healing is correction. Imagining the worst is not correct, so in order to heal, be aware of any thoughts that are not based in reality. Start to think in terms of what is known to be true. Change thoughts that are anxious into true (and balanced) thoughts.

A self-assessment of your thoughts is something you can do. Notice if any of your self-talk includes these phrases: Always, never, perfect, evil, right, wrong, good, bad, nothing, everything. These words are polarised, showing a one-sided belief system.

Being balanced or close to it sees both sides of a situation and reduces the emotional weight you have to carry. When I have been angry at a person for lying, my belief is they are wrong and bad. Anger is a first reaction and is heavy to carry in the body.

Many times, communication has changed my beliefs because I found out more information and showed understanding about where they were coming from. Once again, the **truth lightens the load**. Over time we gain a realistic perspective, even if originally, the situation or person was labelled bad.

Taking in a broader perspective can settle emotions. Beliefs that are rigid and based on false or missing information, slow down progress. When our thoughts are correct and healing action is taken, emotions become balanced, no longer weighed down by heavy judgement.

BALANCED WORRYING

THE EXTREME OPTIMIST:

Things always go perfectly for me. There is nothing to worry about. I don't want to think about the negative. I follow the law of attraction. I believe that thinking positively will make the outcome turn out in my favour. People are generally good and help me get what I want.

This person may be gullible, naïve and get blindsided. Boundaries are used only minimally. They have given up practical awareness and are likely to be taken by surprise.

THE EXTREME PESSIMIST:

Things never go well for me. No matter what I do, it always turns out bad. I have to worry because others are too care-free. Complaining gives me a small relief, especially when people validate my world view. I believe that assuming the worst is realistic. People are generally bad and selfish.

This person will be so negative that they stop taking practical action, seeing no benefit or reward in doing so. Boundaries are over-used which blocks new opportunities. They may feel stuck and trapped in a rigid mindset.

The Balanced Realist:

There will be positives and negatives in this situation. Yin and yang occur simultaneously. I will increase the positive results and put safeguards in place to take care of challenges that could happen. Worry prompts me to be alert. With knowledge and presence, I focus on results and take quality action.

This person is practical, focusing on outcomes and using worry to prepare for the future. Boundaries are used consciously on a case-by-case basis. They are not stuck in either an extreme positive or negative mindset.

Note when you hear people using the following words: always, never, perfect, evil, wrong, good, bad. The person who uses these words will be polarised in their thoughts and emotions. Likely they are exaggerating or minimising reality.

Here are a few statements which are balanced and true. They are free of judgement, either stating truth or taking on a broader perspective. There is no delusion here and therefore a lower emotional reaction.

1. "I am who I am."
2. "Water can hydrate the body."
3. "In a relationship my partner will provide me with support and challenge. I will do the same in return. In my life I will be praised and criticised. I will have many successes and mistakes to learn from on the journey."

Imagining the worst for hours each day is extreme. The nervous system will be distressed. Stress hormones adrenaline and cortisol will be flowing through the blood stream. Worry can be a habit. Something we do automatically, without any process or purpose behind it.

I am offering that your worry can be more conscious. Think of a situation that has been bothering you. Write down your concerns. For each concern write down 3 potential solutions and when you will take action on them. For each concern also jot down a healing perspective – like what is true – free of judgement.

Concern: This surgery could go wrong. I'm scared to lose my family member.

Healing action 1: Ask the medical team questions we've been worried about.

Healing action 2: Follow the surgeon's advice.

Healing action 3: Let family know what is happening and accept support.

Healing perspective: "We have a very good surgeon, and the operation has a 95% success rate. Yes, risks exist but they will not consume my mind. I accept the high likelihood of a healing outcome."

Think thoughts that are:

- True (based on facts)
- Taking into account a wider perspective
- Feeling grounded
- Solution based
- Both positive and negative

Worry is valuable when it leads to action. Let's say in the lead up to surgery a patient is behind on their blood tests. Worry is valid in this case because they are avoiding correct action. Those who get tests done and improve lifestyle, will find peace quicker than those who procrastinate. If worry prompts you to gain knowledge and plan ahead then it has served you well. Once correct action has been undertaken worry is lessened.

Doing what needs to be done is a great stress reliever.

Worry Positives:

- Brings issues to our attention
- Part of the mind's problem-solving process
- Leads to new ideas
- Mindful worrying helps us to be alert and prepared
- Keeps us safe
- Useful when it leads to corrective action

Worry Negatives:

- Sleep disruption
- Can be overwhelming
- Can feel like a trapped mindset
- Decreases mood and productivity
- Worry can affect digestion, immunity and energy
- Can affect mental and physical health

EMOTIONAL ADDICTION

An addiction of drugs/alcohol/food is to avoid pain or gain pleasure. The desire to feel better can be strong but there is no healing effect that takes place. Avoidance is the anxious path, being in the lower-minded amygdala. Not only does an addicted person miss the opportunity to correct thoughts, they damage the body, further increasing anxiety.

Addiction always includes a false reality. Like I need a drink to feel less stress and pain, while the habit consequently poisons their body, disrupts their mind, decreases happiness, leads to illness or injury, messes with their sleep, damages their relationships, numbs emotions or makes them volatile and causes them to not be present with their kids.

Poison is not a healing path. Well-being for body and mind is healing. Don't mistake anxiety's lies for truth. Facing reality is hard however it is the path to be free from anxiety

Now that you see the difference between avoidance and healing you are in a position of power. You can choose a path of presence and healing thoughts. 'Healing truth' is non-addictive and illuminating. Poison is exciting with the fantasy of feeling better, leading to the nightmare of physical and mental illness.

We know that there is no healing via drugs/alcohol/food because there is no correction of thought. If the issue that caused anxiety is lingering, it will resurface and could get even worse. There is no new knowledge, support, action, alignment or truth – which are needed to build confidence.

UNHOOKING FROM SHAME AND PRIDE

No matter what you have done in the past, it is not worth extreme pride nor shame. When prideful we put ourselves on a pedestal and look down on other people. When ashamed we put ourselves down in a hole, looking up at others, believing they are worth more.

All my life I have been unimpressed with pride and avoided shame. Not that I don't feel good serving people and bad when making a mistake, I do. What I mean is that I don't believe living in pride or shame for an extended time is fair on anybody. Learning from a temporary setback is enough.

A self-judgement of pride or shame is witnessing oneself in a limited capacity. You are not that bad, and you are not that good. You are all of yourself, which is the truth. You have had thousands of successes in your life and have contributed to people and this world.

No doubt there have been mistakes too. In some situations, you could have done more but this does not define you. Mistakes are due to a lack of knowledge, being inexperienced or missing support. Other times you put in great effort however it just might not work out.

~~I am a failure.~~

"I am a combination of my unique traits, successes, mistakes, beliefs and actions. I am all of my self, not the limited, bad part anxiety tells me I am."

Expand your definition of self to include all of you. This way you won't be an anxious person scared to show people who you are. When you can stand and say, "I am all of who I am," this is a healing action.

Scenario 1. Doing my best and proud that someone is pleased.

Scenario 2. Doing my best and ashamed that someone is very displeased.

Both of these scenarios have happened to me. The confusion occurred when effort didn't lead to the expected outcome. In scenario 2 I tried much and got poor results. The point here is to focus on what can be controlled, like fairness in the present moment.

It is unfair to measure self-worth based on other's reactions. It is risky for someone else to control what we think of ourselves. Even parents should not have the right to say we are worthy or unworthy. The potential damage is too high in terms of mental health.

Do others think we are good enough? Successful enough? Smart enough? Attractive enough? They should not get to determine this on our behalf.

I'm on record that people do not have the right to comment on someone's self-worth except to help them become realistic about themselves. We can say, "You are all of yourself and that's okay. You are loved."

Along the way people will not understand, or react from their own mental conditioning when labelling us good or bad. Conditions occurring out of our control should not cause us to be rooted in pride or shame. Putting in effort can lead to unpredictable results, including how happy we can make someone.

The desire for that which is unobtainable (only pride) and the desire to avoid the unavoidable (never shame) is the source of human suffering.

A healthy measure of success is to do your best, in alignment with what you care about. Be content with this. A hankering to perfectly please more and more people, will lead to weight and suffering. Better it is to be satisfied with quality work, over time.

ELIZABETH'S WORK

Author Elizabeth Gilbert had to manage her mindset after 'Eat Pray Love' sold 10 million copies. One could easily believe they are amazing, wonderful and gifted. Riding the wave of pride from these massive sales would have been an extreme high, but she was cautious, knowing that from great height, comes a painful fall.

She says and I'm paraphrasing, "I am lucky not to be caught up in the emotion of my writing success and failure. I don't want public opinion to determine how I feel about myself." Elizabeth said, that being entitled to doing her best work is the feeling she allowed herself.

'Committed' was the next book she published, which sold 1/20th of what her best-seller did and had lower review scores. In this circumstance she did not have to spiral into the emotions of shame, despair and failure. Her joyful path was to do her best writing. NOT be responsible for pleasing millions of people.

> *She found her own measurement for enough, which was realistic and about doing her best.*

HIGHER MINDED SELF-VIEW OR LOWER MINDED JUDGEMENT

Lower minded shame lacks the benefits that the whole picture provides. Judgement has us quick to form a conclusion, often from a single thought or small sample of behaviour. Let your basis for reality be far more detailed than that. Healthy self-view is higher minded because it is based on true observation and analysis. Start to assemble evidence of the whole situation.

Even if you had a terrible parent or tough upbringing, the awful words planted in your mind are not you, but they sure do feel like it. This healing opportunity says, be brave to look at those thoughts. Face and stare them down. Demand that only the truth of light remain. "I am all of me, not the voices of others."

A healthy self-esteem does not linger in pride and shame for long, as the illusion is realised. While pride and shame can be felt, they are limited delusions. Remember not to be hooked by positive or negative feelings that only provide half the picture. Take the time to reflect on truth.

> *"By way of preamble let me say that one of the most depressing aspects of so many discussions of self-esteem today is the absence of any reference to the importance of thinking or respect for reality. Too often, consciousness or rationality are not judged to be relevant, since they are not raised as considerations. The notion seems to be that any positive feeling about the self, however arrived at and regardless of its grounds, equals self-esteem."*
> **Nathaniel Branden**

Is reality a consideration in how we view ourselves? If someone works to serve others, at the expense of their well-being, there is a low self-image here, but this person is actually very valuable. The person who puts themselves last should feel amazing about themselves, for the sacrifice and endurance they put in.

Unfortunately, they are delusional in their self-appraisal, always thinking they are not worthy while often they are the kindest of the group. The proud person also has an incorrect self-appraisal, thinking they are so wonderful while not contributing anywhere near the service orientated person does.

STRICT CRITERIA

Worth does not need to be based on extreme standards. Anxiety says only if certain criteria are met, that we worthy of love and self-acceptance. To place strict demands on ourselves is not fair. Anxiety doesn't let us win because it says we are not enough and must be different to qualify.

Self-acceptance can only occur in the present moment. There is no future version of yourself that is more acceptable than you are right now. Start accepting this version of yourself you are now. Self-acceptance is not obtained. It is not achieved. Self-acceptance is practiced.

> *Don't be waiting to accept yourself in the future. The present-moment version of you is the one to love and care for now.*

How often should I practice self-acceptance? Do it every day until it becomes a natural part of your thinking process. Practice while driving or doing housework. While going about your day, praise yourself.

When conditioning yourself to the truth of your self-worth, these will be just words and later you will feel and believe them. The affirmations will become natural to say (because they are). You will think about yourself from a caring place and know your worth.

To create new beliefs in the mind and new neural pathways in the brain, repetition has been shown to dramatically increase benefits. Your path to healing self-worth (out of the cycle of pride and shame) is to accept the present-moment version of yourself. How do you start to do this? Here is a practical healing ritual:

SELF-ACCEPTANCE EXERCISE:

Make a list of the true, valuable aspects of who you are. Write a list of 200 items minimum, how you have provided value to the world. You can write them all at once or come back to add new items over time.

When I first completed this list, I thought, "Geez this is arrogant", but it's not. Arrogance is fake. What we are doing is listing true ways you have acted as a valuable person.

You can start from your time of birth to the present, writing about each time you were valuable to someone. Commit to yourself that you will write at least 200 benefits you have brought to the world. This will rewrite the fictional story of not being enough, into the true story of who you really are.

Make the list about things you have already done. If you made parents smile, scored a goal in soccer, bought someone a present, worked a job, gave money, supported a friend, taught a skill, cooked for loved ones, raised a child, forgave and loved people, include these. Each time you provided value would be an addition to your list.

This list is not minimised for an imaginary audience nor exaggerated to impress people. It is to take ownership of your worth. Write a list that is true. Include times you have worked hard, done your best and been of service to people (even if it was at your job). If you go ahead and write this list, it acts as a healing solution to low self-worth and shame.

Choose 5 things from this list each day and remind yourself of your value. Do this and you will own self-worth. Neither anxiety nor anyone will ever be able to make you believe you are not enough.

Anxiety cannot argue with the reality of your self-worth. Fill the mind with truth!!

Throughout this book I have not said to alter ABC or XYZ in order to accept yourself. My message is that we are okay with ourselves and our difficult emotions. None of these things are wrong. The message is to accept our true selves. We release the imaginary and future version of ourselves, that anxiety tricks us into focusing on.

It is the present moment where your mind must be. Accept the present moment version of yourself. Not avoidance. Not resistance. Just correct, healing thoughts and actions. It is up to you to use healing thoughts now. Your mind will get used to self-acceptance, gratitude and reality. The lightness of these higher thoughts will change how you feel about yourself.

I don't feel proud nor ashamed of my self-worth list. It is just a correct list. A true list of valuable things I've done and anxiety has nothing to say about it. We can tell anxiety, "You don't get a say here. My self-worth is all the valuable things I've done and the ones I can't remember too. Because not everything I've done can be recalled, I am even more valuable than I believe."

GRIEF AND LOSS

Common emotions that accompany grief include:

- **Anxiety.** Be aware of anxious symptoms that often coexist with grief. Excessive worry about others and regret that you could have done more, are common.
- **Anger.** Death, especially if untimely, feels deeply unfair. Post loss may make you angrier than you have been in the past.
- **Despair.** Grief is tough to comprehend, and overwhelm may leave you feeling despair. Remember to reach out to loved ones that are still here.
- **Apathy.** Nothing may feel important compared to your loss. Their passing away was such a shock that other life goals fade to the background.
- **Loneliness.** The grieving often isolate themselves and feel alone in their mourning. It may feel like no one understands what you're going through.
- **Low energy.** You may be sleeping more or less than usual, and catch yourself sighing deeply and feeling generally fatigued.

SUBCONSCIOUS ANXIOUS BELIEFS

I remember hearing about survivor's guilt as a young child. It intrigued me that a person would take on blame for something they were not at fault for. A passenger who survived a car crash for example, would blame themselves. "If only I hadn't made us 10 minutes late, none of this would have happened," they might say.

Logically we know that leaving late is not the cause of the collision but anxiety will fool us into taking on full blame. Crashes are contributed to by driver error, inattention, speed, uneven road surface (pot holes), vehicle malfunction, weather and other factors.

Anxiety increases certain emotions like grief by finding blame in situations that aren't warranted. In the process of healing, it is advantageous to reflect on emotions and the subconscious beliefs behind them.

Do those with survivor's guilt have a tendency towards guilt in general? Is it because they have an exaggerated level of responsibility? Is it because they felt lost after their loved ones passing and guilt was something to hold onto? In any case, surviving does not equal blame and we must remain fair in our self-appraisal.

There are a variety of anxious beliefs that could surface during times of grief and rejection. Be conscious of these beliefs and utilise healing truth when appropriate.

Should have known this would happen. This anxious belief has us being hard on ourselves for being unaware of something that we could not have known. Perhaps a loved one did not reveal the severity of an illness they had. It is not our responsibility to guess what other people are going through. Don't be unfair on yourself, striving for impossible standards.

Action step in the present moment: Reflect on the quality of communication with loved ones now. Can communication be clearer in your marriage and family? Can loved ones be prompted for transparency? We have a right to ask for this.

I'm never going to be happy again. Only anxiety thinks in terms of never and always. We should not place a limit on our ability to feel good again nor pressure to heal quickly. It is best to embody our feelings in the present moment whether they be negative, positive, or both. If you cry at the memory of a loved one, that's okay. If you have tears of joy and laughter, that too is okay.

Action step in the present moment: Let your expression of emotion be natural. Resisting feelings is an anxious path. Instead, express your feelings by crying, writing, talking or another healing outlet. Freedom of expression is a human right.

I have to be strong. We may feel the need to be perfectly composed during the grieving process. Perfectionism is anxiety 101. We may feel a need to hold it together for everyone else. It is important to acknowledge your needs and feelings too. This is healthy self-esteem.

Action step in the present moment: Give support to those around you and be sure to accept emotional, financial and practical support from others too. Accepting no support is an anxious protection mechanism.

I didn't say I love you enough. Thoughts like I could have said I love you more, or I wish I hadn't said nasty things are anxious thoughts. Sure, you could have said more, but it did not eventuate. There were reasons for that. They may have had a difficult personality or knew there was a loving connection without saying it.

Action step in the present moment: Call and spend time with loved ones who are still here. Let them know they are special to you. We can't change past mishaps, but correct action now can mean the world to someone.

Could have prevented their death if I was there. This belief is not fair on you. Death at best can be delayed but is a part of life, which is important for us to accept. 'What ifs' are anxious imaginings. If you visit thoughts of rescuing those who have passed, remind yourself that you cared and that is all that could have been done. Might they have been saved? No one can know for certain.

Action step in the present moment: Collect your thoughts and breathe. Affirm: "I am here. I am now. I look after myself and others." Be as present as you can be, there is less anxiety here.

Fear of losing more people. Be grateful for loved ones passed and those who are still here now. It is unknown whether others will leave us in years or decades, those you are worried about losing, visit and connect with them regularly. This is an action you do now. See if you can switch your fear into present moment love.

Action step in the present moment: Think of family and friends you can express love to. Call on their birthday and send messages to whom might be uplifted. When the thought of not loving enough enters the mind, perform a loving gesture.

TIMELINE GRATITUDE PROCESS

I awoke at 3:00am inspired to do this healing process. I leant a pillow against the wall and sat up in bed. I thought of every significant person from my birth to the present day. I found gratitude for meaningful school friends, teachers, parents, stepparents, grandparents, cousins, family, workmates, girlfriends, mentors, strangers, healers and adult friends.

For the next 90 minutes I recalled how each person had made a difference in my life, big and small. I thought about support that was given, special moments, fun, joyful laughter and deep connections.

I made sure to be truly grateful for each person before moving on to the next.

My heart filled with love. More than that, I felt love throughout my timeline. I cried and laughed several times. Over 150 people had contributed to me and I felt deep inside that I had no loneliness anymore. At every stage of my life, love was there.

Be in a quiet space and allow yourself the time. Start at the beginning and progress year by year. Think of all the special people you have met. Recall those who contributed to your upbringing, education and life. Those who helped with well-being, health, family, career, finance, intimacy, cooking, holidays, sport, artists, authors, musicians, spiritual teachers, children, animals, people you loved and who loved you.

I have been unlucky and suffered heartache. I found my father passed away when I was 16 years old and the next year my friend took his own life. I've had 4 missed opportunities to be a father. I have spent long periods of time away from family and 10 years single, living alone as an adult.

There is a human tendency to not notice our blessings unless we focus on them. Being grateful is a state you can be in. This healing process is asking you to go there. We might think that we were alone during a certain time period yet when we look, somebody was there. This process works because of a special truth. Universal love provides.

Like any skill we must practice, to get better.

When I found out that I was not the father to my son, I missed him. The dynamic of parent/child still played out for me though. I remained part of his life for several years and later I was a school bus driver of 50 kids. In every 'lonely' moment a special person was actually there. Those who go to prison speak of this; a cellmate, guard, friend or even a bird will be there. Or they find God, spirituality and community that is meaningful for them.

What I am missing will be carried out by someone else but not always in an expected way. Love doesn't provide the person I want, in the way I expect. Life (universal love) does provide though. Unexpectedly a person, pet or even wild animal will connect with us at a deeper level, at the time we need it.

ACKNOWLEDGING SADNESS AND JOY

Would I suggest being present with sadness? Yes, fully experiencing an emotion is cathartic. A great cry can even include relief or laughter, when sadness and joy come together in remembrance. A light heart after expression is a sign you embodied your emotions.

Resisting and avoiding feelings will make our troubles last longer. Natural expression is a healing action. All feelings are valid yet we can make sure not to get stuck in a pattern of emotion, like grief or sadness.

I have felt every emotion there is and will again in the future but I make sure that my mindset is realistic and present. The feeling is quite real yet the beliefs that emotion is based on are often incomplete.

Acknowledge your emotion and the belief that goes with it. I don't recommend changing the feeling but to be mindful with your self-talk. Correct beliefs that are including never, always, past, future, nothing, forever, terrible, perfect, should haves and what ifs. These absolutes are not part of a realistic mindset.

An emotion that is expressed and then unhooked from anxiety is released swiftly.

The truth is everyone has their own pace in healing from a big life event. Should someone be judged if they fully move past their grief? To judge someone for living happily again is unfair. This book suggests that we allow the possibility of healing rather than thinking there will be no recovery.

Is it wrong to enjoy life again soon? I asked myself this after my father passed away. The answer was clear, he would want me to be happy. He wouldn't want me to pay a debt of sadness. Instead, I could embody whichever emotions are present and keep him in my heart.

Both happy and sad, grief and relief, pleasure and pain occur together. Human beings experience a balance of emotions. Being present with this reality is part of healing anxiety. A balanced perspective on people, emotions and life will cause you no loss of sleep.

CONCLUSION

STEVE'S SELF-CARE

Steve had so many preventable things creating anxiety, that I told him this is a good thing. "You can improve in any area and life will get better."

Steve had dozens of thoughts and habits misaligned for a healthy mindset. So much was out of balance that it was easy to see why anxiety had taken hold. Steve had a passion for classic cars and wanted a relationship, which he didn't believe would even be possible in his current state.

Steve was anxious and felt worthless. He procrastinated and was unfulfilled. He worked a lot but had no savings. Many coffees and energy drinks were consumed yet he was fatigued. This was his situation. He also had trouble sleeping, skipped meals, smoked cigarettes and drank alcohol daily. There was more but you get the picture.

A lack of enthusiasm for life, meant physical and mental health were in decline. Steve used several coffees to power on during the day, then alcohol and medication to switch off at night.

Me: "There are a number of things out of balance, which also means there are several ways you can start to feel better quite quickly.

HEALING ANXIETY

Switching from habits that are causing anxiety, to rituals that promote wellness will serve you greatly.

Positive lifestyle rituals will create a healing path for you. Let's begin with 3 small time blocks dedicated to your well-being. At times when you used to down coffee, smoke cigarettes or procrastinate, use these new rituals instead. They don't take too long.

The philosophy is that by giving your body and mind what is truly needed, some bad habits will fall away completely and others will lessen. I have seen this outcome occur thousands of times, with healing rituals in place."

- Morning 30 Minutes: Prepare for the day by setting an intention for self-care. First actions are suggested to be body movement, water and a hot breakfast. As you are a coffee drinker, only consume this afterwards.
- Lunch 30 Minutes: Use this time to give your body and mind a rest from work. Collect your thoughts, stretch your legs and eat quality food. Breaks refresh the mind and enhance wellness.
- Evening 30 Minutes: Use evening rituals to slow down from daily stimulation. Write 5 things you are grateful for. Meditation is recommended to relax the nervous system. In doing so, you give body and mind a chance to settle before bed.

"It is the time dedicated to self-care consistently that makes a difference. We use our thoughts and body to create well-being and heal anxiety. It happens through daily practices. Just as you can DO anxiety (causing it to be), you can also DO healing (causing better outcomes through thoughts and actions).

I haven't forgotten about your coffee. It is not expected that you quit, when you were having 10 cups of International Roast per day. My suggestion is to have caffeinated drinks only after the morning ritual of water, walking and food. Consider lowering your coffee intake to 1-2 cups per day.

You will be deriving vitality from the 3 rituals. These rituals are a guide and you can adjust them as needed. You can make them longer or include other rewarding options, like mindful breathing, nature and music to name a few. Caffeine overstimulation probably contributed to anxiety and sleep problems. You deserve habits that renew your energy, metabolism and well-being."

CARS, RESPECT AND MONEY

Steve's primary occupation was truck driving and he also restored classic cars. This used to be a passion however recently it felt like a burden. Steve received restoration jobs from friends and acquaintances but wasn't charging much money – some weren't paying him at all.

Steve: "I have several small car jobs to complete but I'm procrastinating. More people are asking for help too and I can't keep up with demand. It's a bit of a mess. I am still owed money from previous work and barely make enough to get by."

Me: "Okay, let's break down what is happening into smaller parts."

Me: "Would you say that you are charging a fair amount to your customers?"

Steve: "Too fair. I charge half of what other professionals do for the same work. I give pretty big discounts."

Me: "I hear you aren't receiving much money for restoration and paint work on these classic cars and some owners haven't paid at all."

Steve: "Yeah, there are a few I'm still waiting on." He laughed (I estimated from his resigned chuckle, this has happened several times).

Me: "What is the longest you have been stiffed on an agreed price?"

Steve: "2 years. And he still hasn't paid."

Me: "Are you procrastinating because you aren't getting paid a fair price? I'll bet a few of these jobs are from friends who expect you will work for next to nothing? Are you alcohol binging for reward because you feel cheated and unsatisfied at the moment?"

HEALING ANXIETY

Steve nodded: "Yes, yes and yes. I never thought about it like that."

Me: "It is time you get a fair deal. My vision for you is an increase in your money, time, energy and peace of mind. Steep discounts and not getting paid at all, rob you of these. Start charging what the work is worth and take payment upfront for your valuable skills.

Consider making a one-page business plan. This will bring much needed reward to your passion of car detailing and restoration. Make the plan simple, fitting on a single A4 size page. If others charge $800, then your price can be between $700-900. Perhaps the rate of $700 for full payment up front and $900 on payment plan. Of course, projects will vary, adjust to suit the actual job requirements."

I offered suggestions that are fair for him and the customer, based on the healthy self-esteem principle – both parties are taken care of:

1. Clear current workload before taking on additional jobs.
2. Let new customers know about the updated pricing structure.
3. State pricing options. Don't discount further.
4. Apply the new pricing model. Example: $700 upfront or $900 with a $450 deposit.
5. Those following a payment plan are required to pay a deposit.
6. Let customers know why payment is needed. i) Ordering replacement parts and paint is costly ii) Sourcing rare items is time consuming. iii) It has been unfair in the past, paying out of your own pocket and people have taken advantage. iv) Your skill has been honed over two decades.
7. Take on jobs with A-grade clients. People who complain about your boundaries can be referred elsewhere.
8. Include three 30-minute self-care rituals in your day. Morning, afternoon and evening.

Me: "Charging a fair amount will agitate those wanting to take advantage of you. This is good. Genuine customers (and friends) will respect your time and value. The goal is fairness for customer and operator. How would it feel to not chase people for money again?"

I asked Steve to consider the following questions. The purpose of this is to find a healing perspective and support an empowered mindset:

- What are the wonderful qualities you have?
- Can you charge a fair amount to customers?
- Would you feel better about yourself if friends didn't rip you off?
- Can you accept that some might be unhappy when you charge more?

Steve's response: "I'm such a failure."

Me: "Failure is very hard to achieve. Even partial failure is difficult. No! You must have ceased trying entirely, we know that's not true because here you are in my office right now. You must have learnt nothing from the past but that's not the case either. Your actions must have produced no benefit for yourself and others. We know this is not true, as you are a skilled operator."

Me: "Say I have had temporary challenges that I am now overcoming. Completing things gives me satisfaction." Silence from Steve.

Me: "I mean Steve, say these words please."

Steve: "I have had temporary challenges that I am now overcoming. Completing things gives me satisfaction… I'm not a failure actually I've just been in a rut."

In no uncertain terms we must stop DOING anxiety, in order to stop FEELING anxiety. **Our thoughts and actions matter**. If you compelled someone who thinks they are a failure to list all their successes, you would be listening to them for hours.

Failure is simply a limited perception of reality. To heal anxiety, train your mind to be honest and accurate about life and yourself. Most problems are temporary. Most negative beliefs are made up without a second thought for confirmation. We can think truthful thoughts to heal our mindset and self-esteem.

Steve went on to implement recommendations that improved health and settled his nervous system.

- Changed his self-talk from 'I'm failing' to 'I'm learning about my mind now.'
- Completed jobs that were previously procrastinated on for 5 months.
- Quit smoking with the WARP (Walker Addiction Removal Process) and reduced coffee.

BLUE PILL, RED PILL

In the Matrix movie, characters choose between 2 pills, leading to either a restricted or illuminated version of reality. The blue pill represents staying within the confines of a simulation, consequently never discovering reality. Those who swallow the blue pill stay in illusion, unconsciously limited yet familiar to them.

Ultimately the blue pill means being ruled by pleasure and pain, fantasy and fear. They are unsatisfied from the system that restricts and controls them but compulsively feed on reward from that same system, like a mouse pressing the food button in its cage. A little hit of dopamine reward is enough to distract from its prison, for a while.

Think obsessively drinking alcohol despite feeling sick, or an OCD hoarder collecting more garbage, as real-world examples of pressing the dopamine button to distract from an anxious prison. "I need more." The anxious ritual is done to feel-better-in-prison, which of course feels awful. Everybody knows truth is important, but a little anxious voice says, take the garbage blue pill.

The illusionary Matrix tempts us with indulgence, drama and judgement. It does not offer sobering truth. Realisation of truth is actually evolution for human beings. A person will only progress once they release their current state of delusion.

The red pill represents freedom. Those who take the red pill, desire reality and are prepared to leave illusion behind. They accept there are challenges in dealing with the real world. They value truth which equates to freedom. Choosing this path means being responsible for one's healing journey. There is nobody 'out there' to blame anymore.

The Matrix will still tempt us with a false reality. Being free and empowered requires maintenance. The mind must be regularly fed premium fuel (true thoughts). The healing path is fuelled by this motivation to reclaim control of reality.

A mind operating free from illusion, does not continue spinning in circles pretending the simulation is real. They have escaped the trap and do well to discern between fact and fiction. They still have stress, like everybody else but ultimately create their own experience.

AUTHENTIC HEALING

There are several good reasons to be authentic and top of this list is a chance to heal. Telling people that you have anxiety shines a light of truth on the situation. Anxiety that is kept inside reinforces itself whereas letting the cat out of the bag has many benefits.

We might think telling people will be **bad**. Not true. There will be positive and negative consequences. Telling people makes me **not enough** or weak. No. Revealing your truth shows strength and self-acceptance. After I tell people they will **reject** me. Not true. The right people will stay by your side however if a few leave, this says more about their character than yours.

Reasons to tell trusted people you have been dealing with anxiety and are working on healing.

- You let go of built-up emotional energy. You are taking a load of tension off your mind, chest and shoulders.
- When people know your triggers, they can make adjustments to accommodate. A simple change that successfully avoids an anxiety attack is a great result.

- When others understand what you are going through, they offer appropriate care. They can start helping you.
- People will support you by saying you are worthy. You are okay. The real you is enough. You are loved.
- Those around you get to live in the real world by your side, knowing the truth.
- When secrets are revealed, healing begins for you and others. It only happens once the truth comes out and all are living in reality.
- You release the fear of people finding out by simply telling them. We either live in fear of an illusion or engage with reality which will keep us sane.

By hiding feelings, we live with a degree of pretending. Pretending everything is fine and that our needs are not important. The other person by consequence of us hiding anxiety, doesn't get the chance to understand us. They remain confused and frustrated.

Maybe you don't want people fussing over you 24 hours a day once they know you have anxiety. The good news is you can ask for the type of support you want. It could be something simple like, "Be patient with me while I gather my thoughts. I need space for an hour. I don't need you to do anything. Just understand and I'll be good to go."

Open communication about healing anxiety means you get to ask for more of what you want. This is a wonderful opportunity to live authentically. I can tell you from personal experience that when needs are shared with others, it opens up more healing, not less. Just having someone else understand what you are going through is a relief.

Consider that by keeping anxious thoughts all inside, what you are missing out on. A chance to be heard and cared for. A chance for new perspectives and practical solutions.

Anxiety might say, "Why tell them they don't care about me

anyway?" The truth is if you have not told people, then you have never truly been cared for. Because no one knows what you are going through they are limited in being there for you emotionally. I want you to have this opportunity.

It is true that some will be better equipped to handle your feelings than others. This fact does not mean zero healing potential. A few will be terrific at helping you manage anxiety. Start with the people you believe are capable of helping. Work closely with your psychologist and hypnotherapist too.

Keep in mind that after telling someone you have anxiety, they might not immediately register what that means. The built-up emotion is something you have lived with for years or decades. Others will need a minute to catch up to your level of awareness and they don't have to understand every little detail in order to be helpful.

Telling someone is not a one-time event. I suggest having ongoing conversations to update on emotions and mental health. A period of adjustment may be needed, as all come to terms with this new reality. A weekly topic of discussion that leads to progress is quite appropriate. Talk about what did and did not work, in terms of healing.

What I confessed, made me blessed.

Do you feel you could tell people you are healing anxiety? What difference would it make if you did?

WAITING TO HEAL

A study by Christian Jarrett of the British Psychological Society concluded that out of 9000 mental health patients, only 1/3 thought that therapy/psychology services could help them. On average it took 10.5 years before admitting to having a problem and then 4-6 months to seek assistance.

'Anxiety, panic attacks and other mental health issues can't wait. During uncertain times your mental well-being is more important than ever and waiting until life gets back to normal is not a guaranteed solution. Avoidance generally makes symptoms worse.'

Healing-based therapy helps to raise awareness, think productively, find solutions and figure out our truth. When going through something challenging reach out for assistance. Waiting for problems to resolve themselves is risky because that anxiety could last for years or even a lifetime.

STILL WAITING

"Time will tell." This little phrase is for people who prefer leaving results to the passage of time. Whether it's because they don't know how to start healing or that life is overwhelming, our mental health deserves better than random chance to fix ever worsening anxiety.

If you are thirsty, is it better to drink now or wait until dehydrated? If unsafe, is it better to leave quickly or remain in danger? If unhappy, is it better to do what you love now or remain unfulfilled for another year? And if anxious, is it better to engage in healing now or wait, leaving thoughts and beliefs uncorrected?

Whilst hope is important, it is not a strategy. Those suffering most internalise their problems to the point of despair. We must break the habit of *waiting* to feel better. To heal we must use a variety of healing tools, in the present moment.

Knowledge + Support + Action = A Load off of Your Mind.

FOUNDATIONS OF MASTERING ANXIETY

KNOWLEDGE

Gaining information contributes to confidence. With understanding we are empowered to make better decisions and control our destiny. Without knowledge, anxiety fills in the unknown with doubts, worries and imagination.

Taking Action
Finishing tasks give feelings of accomplishment in the present. We don't have to 'think about things' that are complete. Quality actions made with knowledge, is wisdom. Procrastination and avoiding responsibility are anxious responses.

Asking for Support
By getting help, you are expressing that anxiety is occurring and it is your mission to heal. Anxiety keeps us hidden away, missing an opportunity for healing. Getting support from a person you are safe and comfortable with, is an act of reclaiming power.

Intention Setting
Setting an intention each day gives direction to your subconscious mind. In doing so you are influencing your frame of mind. For example, my mission is to be present. If the mind drifts off to the past or future, then my intention re-focuses me on here and now.

A Sense of Safety
Being safe must be the number one priority. At home and work, feeling unsafe is a major cause of anxiety. Having been through trauma, the mind will build a wall to keep out perceived dangers, both real and imagined. Be safe and look after one another.

Fairness
Being selfish misses caring for other's needs. Being selfless misses looking after oneself. Fairness is love, where all are taken care of (including you). A fair person recognises the value of others and themselves. Both giving and receiving are part of healthy interactions.

Mindfulness
The quality of breathing, self-talk and general mental health can fall under mindful attention. Awareness of thought patterns that

are useful vs not useful, is a sign of mastery. I encourage mindful attention of your thoughts, beliefs and nervous system.

REDUCING OVERWHELM
A life full of stress means we have taken on too much. The nervous system is frazzled and overwhelmed. Creating a balanced lifestyle with space to think, rest and enjoy ourselves is important. When more relaxed in general we tend to sleep better too.

QUALITY SLEEP
Safety, mindfulness techniques and reducing anxiety help improve sleep. Making rest a priority is imperative. Small changes really can make a great difference to sleep quality. With proper rest we are more likely to improve mood, energy and mental clarity.

SELF-ACCEPTANCE
An integrated person accepts all that is unique about themselves, including: strengths, abilities, personality traits and desires. This also means accepting limitations, mistakes, weaknesses and shadow side.

SOCIAL CONFIDENCE
Being comfortable with socialising, dating and job interviews allows us more opportunities and expression. We all want to feel at ease, so we can enjoy the best things in life. Social confidence means self-acceptance and much less worry about what others *might* be thinking about us.

CREATING A BALANCED MIND AND LIFE
It is time to 'get real' about: mental health, physical health, marriage, money, sex, family, food, travel, exercise, career and self-esteem. No situation is all good, there are challenges. No situation is all bad, there are blessings. Expectations outside of reality, are fantasies and nightmares that make us anxious.

Reality

If your mind is believing that imagination is reality, you've got an anxious pest living upstairs. Double check that your thoughts are as factual as possible. Ask several times each day, "What is definitely true in this situation?" Do your best to stop focusing on the unknown and imagination. Keep tuning into truth.

Alignment

When relationships, work environment and lifestyle are right for you, confidence is higher. When aligned there is less anxiety. Picture a relationship where both partners agree on their financial plan and follow-through. Imagine a workplace with fair pay and the job is rewarding. These are examples of alignment.

Integration and Healing

To be an integrated person is the final step in recovering from anxiety. Your positive and negative thoughts are each part of the whole mind. Both positive and negative are seen as useful but not true. A recovered person will still feel emotions, including anxiety. We don't fight or avoid that fact, rather continue thinking quality thoughts and taking healing actions.

If at some point in the future you have an anxious episode, don't judge it. Let it flow through and away from you. Following the healing steps will facilitate this. It is actually a huge win to reverse an anxious episode. Rather than anxiety lasting weeks or months, perhaps you can settle it down within a few minutes or an hour.

Use your bodily actions to activate your restful nervous system (parasympathetic).

Reflect on the beliefs that lead to anxiety. Affirm true and healing beliefs in their place.

By thinking better, we feel better.

Every thought counts.

www.ingramcontent.com/pod-product-compliance
Lightning Source LLC
Chambersburg PA
CBHW051427290426
44109CB00016B/1458